epic lincolnshire

emusic.

ECOLABOR

HILLSBORO PUBLIC LIBRARIES
Hillsboro, OR
Member of Washington County
COOPERATIVE LIBRARY SERVICES

RECYCLING & REDESIGNING LOGOS

RECYCLING & REDESIGNING LOGOS

A DESIGNER'S GUIDE TO REFRESHING & RETHINKING DESIGN

BEVERLY MASSACHUSETTS

ROCKPORT PUBLISHERS

MICHAEL HODGSON

WITH MATTHEW PORTER

First published in the United States of America by
Rockport Publishers, a member of
Quayside Publishing Group
100 Cummings Center
Suite 406-L
Beverly, Massachusetts 01915-6101
Telephone: (978) 282-9590
Fax: (978) 283-2742
www.rockpub.com

Library of Congress Cataloging-in-Publication Data
Hodgson, Michael.
 Recycling and redesigning logos : a designer's guide to refreshing and rethinking design / Michael Hodgson with Matthew Porter.
    p. cm.
 Includes index.
 ISBN-13: 978-1-59253-611-5
 ISBN-10: 1-59253-611-5
 1. Logos (Symbols)--Design. I. Porter, Matthew. II. Title. III. Title: Designer's guide to refreshing and rethinking design.
 NC1002.L63H63 2010
 741.6--dc22

                                                                 2010014333
                                                                 CIP

ISBN-13: 978-1-59253-611-5 4493 8776 ¼
ISBN-10: 1-59253-611-5

10 9 8 7 6 5 4 3 2 1

Design: Ph.D, A Design Office, www.phdla.com

Photographer credits: Iwan Baan/www.iwan.com, 90, 95; Tim Brown, 154, 155; Michael Hodgson, 8, 47, 91, 93; Peter Schiazza, 126; Sarah Sears, 152; Ann Sherman, 153; Parker Smith, 102; Mario Testino 71; Graham Watson, 162

Printed in China

This book is dedicated to my father, Leslie Hodgson—
a lovely man and a loving husband, father, and grandfather who left too soon
and who believed that there was one more deadly sin.

ANGER COVETOUSNESS SLOTH PRIDE. LUST ENVY GLUTTONY NO SENSE OF HUMOUR

CONTENTS

The Unbearable Likeness of Bean

WHEN MY DAUGHTERS WERE YOUNGER, I'd run with them in our tandem jogger where I live, in Topanga, California, a rural community in the Santa Monica Mountains. The beauty of this area is not only its natural splendor but also the absence of chains. On the final stretch to our "shack in the woods" one day, Maudie Rae, about three then, leaned out of the baby jogger and said, "Look Daddy, Starbucks!" pointing to a crumpled-up Starbucks cup beside the road. I was horrified not only by the litter, but more that it was Starbucks, the behemoth crushing local coffee shops all over the world. But my horror and disappointment were even greater because I realized little Maudie Rae almost instinctively recognized the Starbucks logo. I thought I had "protected" her by living in this beautiful, chain-free community. The power of a logo was never so clearly demonstrated to me.

Zucky's Delicatessen Coffee Shop was a perfect example of the architectural style that became known as Googie. It stood empty for many years after it sadly closed in 1993. Luckily, it was recognized for its significance as a fine local example of this style, and the Santa Monica Historic Preservation Commission designated the Zucky's Restaurant pylon sign as a local city landmark in 2005. Now the building houses the local office of First Republic Bank, whose traditional style signage is somewhat dwarfed by its '60s predecessor.

We interact with logos daily. Some represent new products, interactions, and experiences. Others are long familiar, representing comfort foods or coveted products dating back to childhood. They can be metaphors for benchmarks—our first computer, first car, first utility bill, or first child. Others are steeped in family history, a brand of chocolate chips in our grandmother's cookie.

A logo expresses a visual personality. It conveys the essential persona of a product or a service. It can be welcoming. It can be a promise. It can convey confidence or bravado. Seductively, the logo weaves itself into our emotional landscape. It is both an asset and a veiled liability. Our attachments represent commitments, messy emotional investments. Logos are loaded with potential pitfalls: tread lightly. It must be observed and calibrated to maintain its connection with its intended audience.

Time marches on. Symbols change meaning. Life's events create new associations. New products come, old ones disappear. New technologies inspire innovative solutions and generate new delivery systems. It is a mutating landscape in which even the best logos eventually require rethinking, redesign—or simply refreshing. This book explores the paradoxes involved in determining when and how much change is necessary in order to arrive at a, hopefully, more captivating and enduring visual personality for the first time.

It's easy to decry the power of the logo—that damn Starbuck's cup on the side of my road. Sure, they matter. Logos are born, get nurtured, flourish and grow. If managed creatively and honestly, they can live in harmony with us—and our children, too.

SECTION I

CHAPTER 1
A Refresher Course

A LOGO IS JUST THE START OF THE STORY. A good logo—or sometimes simply a familiar one—is visually arresting and symbolically potent. It sums up the company or organization it represents … which is exactly why it's just the start.

The personal associations a logo calls up normally aren't apparent in the visual symbol itself. The Coca-Cola logo pulls some emotional triggers for everyone— positive and/or negative depending upon whom you ask—but the emotional content of that response isn't just in the familiar flowing script.

I was a Coca-Cola collector as teenager growing up in England. I gathered bottles and bits of ephemera from around the world. I have not enjoyed Coca-Cola much since I was that teenager (and that's a few years ago now), but there remains a link between the Coke look, its contoured bottle, the familiar script, the red, and that syrupy drink. Once every five years or so I try it, if only to remind myself of that taste and my memories and associations. Such is the definition of a good logo: it transcends design by creating an emotional connection between the symbol and your personal story. Between you and it.

In a favorable state, these connections evoke warm feelings and a sense of belonging. Today, we think of these personal connections, held by "consumers," people, as the essence of a brand.

The sum total of the brand experience is "Visual Personality." A successful visual personality captures the emotional attributes of a brand and becomes its personality.

VISUAL PERSONALITY

A brand, then, is the sum of all the connections and shared experiences, feelings, and associations held by stakeholders like customers, employees, shareholders, etc. Sometimes the associations can be bad: think Enron, Exxon, Edsel. But let's not talk about the bad stuff. We are here to talk about successful brands and the associations they hold. What happens when change requires the redesign of a logo or mark so that such brands stay current and connected to new audiences while keeping the existing base?

At Ph.D, we call the sum total of the brand experience "Visual Personality." A successful visual personality captures the emotional attributes of a brand and becomes its personality. Just like someone you know and love. Personality is the trait that attracts you

Do the Math. The sum of all experiences of a brand is its "visual personality." A successful visual personality captures the emotional attributes of a brand and becomes its symbol—the emblem of its products, services, and people.

to them: its gentleness, its concern, its intelligence, its wit, its historical connection to your life, its integrity. As designers, we control visual personality, which includes the logo and the logotype. But it is much more than that. Take a look at UPS and its signature "brown." That is a huge part of its visual personality—the UPS logo is brown, the trucks are brown, and the drivers wear brown. Brown is also used in the company's advertising, and it appeared in the company's tagline and advertising, ("What can brown do for you?"—but that is soon changing).

Visual personality is a specific kind of identity. First, it is visual, but it can be a word, such as a logo coupled with a tagline, slogan, or typographic identifier. Or, in the case of a logotype (or wordmark), it may be just words or letters. But, it is always visual.

A visual personality in a sense points all the way back into a brand's amorphous nature. A well-managed visual personality summons positive associations and warm emotions, and packages them in a visual capsule. The term *logo* is often used to describe a single symbol or mark that embodies a

> "When a redesign is successful, it retains equity from the past, instills it with new meaning in order to position the client or product for future growth."

visual personality. But logos are often designed as families, in a range of sizes, applications, or colors that function as a single system.

Visual personalities often include signature colors. They include words—think of Verizon's classic "Can you hear me now?" tagline that became a part of everyday lexicon. Visual personalities can include audible cues—"Zoom-zoom," from Mazda's personality, and those of us "of a certain age" know Alka-Seltzer "Plop, plop, fizz, fizz" jingle and sound. Visual personalities can be people or animals: Michael Jordon for Nike, Karl Malden for American Express, Geico's Gecko, or AFLAC's duck.

THE CHICKEN OR THE EGG?

When a product or organization is new, it is in an egg stage. A new brand gives us a clean slate, and if the product pleases, positive associations accumulate. A brand is hatched, and we start to build brand equity.

The same thing happens with a new visual personality. By signaling a positive visual image, the public associates the visual personality with their experiences, and equity accumulates.

But this book isn't about new brands or new visual personalities. This book is about refreshing and revitalizing. Evolution and revolution. What characteristics of a brand's visual personality are valuable (have equity)? Which do not? What do you keep? What do you toss? When do you make subtle change—and when must you make wholesale change? When a redesign is successful, it retains equity from the past, instills it with new meaning in order to position the client or product for future growth.

So what *is* the Coca-Cola visual personality? Why did this young lad collect those bottles and retain an association with the brand long after he had stopped sipping its intoxicating sweetness? Was it the name? The Spenserian script? The red? Or the long-tracking shot pulling back to reveal a multicultural group of young people lip-syncing, "I'd like to teach the world to sing …" on an Italian hilltop? My answer: all of these. The sum of its visual personality still resonates with me. I like Coca-Cola's personality. It reminds me of happy times as a skinny youth in Greece with my uncle. Maybe I should try Coke Zero!

PROCESS MAKES PERFECT

DESIGN: SPRING ADVERTISING
VANCOUVER, BRITISH COLUMBIA

LOGO REDESIGNS RANGE FROM tune-ups and refreshes to blue-sky reimaginings. Designers often flatter themselves with the notion that the blue-sky stuff is the usual work. "We started from scratch," or "We didn't keep anything from the old system," they say.

But the truth is that there's almost always some sort of carryover, and that most redesigns can't succeed without knowing what to keep. Unless the client in question has been remarkably bereft of design direction, there's always something that resurfaces in a logo. It might be a tagline or a typographic style; it might be an intangible asset that arises from the consumer's emotional dialogue with the product.

Spring, of Vancouver, British Columbia, is a full-service advertising and design agency, but its design team has developed specialized systems when it comes to logo redesigns. In the few years since they started, they've refined a four-step process that's a wonder of its kind. It achieves simplicity without shallowness:

1. Define the goals. What's happening with the client that makes a new logo necessary?
2. Market study. Who are the customers? Who are the competitors? What are they doing?
3. Articulate the personality. If the product were a person, what would it be like?
4. Develop the identity.

The principals of Spring Advertising are industry veterans who understand the value of a well-written client brief and the importance of knowing how much to retain in the new logo. Design director Perry Chua elaborates: "The brief dictates our approach: Are we repositioning the company? Has there been a merger or acquisition? Is this simply a refresh of the identity?"

Blue sky is wonderful, of course, but so is solid ground.

TALK 1410AM
The Buzz of Vancouver

Well Grounded. Spring's four-step process is fair, accurate, honest, and complete. It leads to creative strategies that lead to effective solutions. Their work for Talk 1410 AM in Vancouver wasn't brain surgery, but it was very smart. (Before: below, After: above)

DEFINE THE GOALS: ONE PROCESS, MANY LOGOS: TALK 1410

Talk 1410, a Vancouver radio station, is a prime example of the value of working through step 1 of Spring's process. The station was changing its name and seeking a new audience, younger and hipper, without losing its more mature listening base.

"You instantly turn an object into a topic of discussion by simply applying the quote marks."

The creatives at Spring conceived of an identity with a built-in marketing advantage. "The redesign strategy aimed to deliver the station with more than just a logo redesign," says Chua. "We wanted to give the client a creative platform from which their personality could be expressed."

The palette is black and white—in Chua's words, "because talk radio is about opinions, which are black and white: you either agree with something

or you don't." The station's tagline, "The Buzz of Vancouver," was retained. But the addition of quote marks within the logo sent a new message: that listening to Talk 1410 would enable listeners to "be quotable—to have an opinion about what people are talking about at the coffee shop."

The clever visual of the quote marks, moreover, was calculated to offer lots of opportunities for guerilla

marketing. When placed around objects or buildings, the quote marks indicate "talked about" status while at the same time reinforcing a visual association with Talk 1410. Capitalizing on issues that are on Vancouver's mind, the quote marks serve as concrete symbols of the radio station's attentive connection to the life of the city. It's an ingenious way of delivering a rich, attractive message: tune into this station, because it's tuned into Vancouver.

"You instantly turn an object into a topic of discussion by simply applying the quote marks," Chua explains, noting that they've been applied to gas prices posted at service stations, the Vancouver Olympics countdown clock, even the entrances of the city's safe injection houses during a discussion of drugs and communicable disease. The Talk 1410 mark, he concludes, illustrates "the difference between what a logo is and what a logo can do for you."

Talking Heads. The addition of the quote marks to the logo was intended to send a message: listening to Talk 1410 will inform your opinions and make you as quotable as any talking head on the radio. The device was also used in guerrilla marketing and advertising to "great effect."

MARKET STUDY

LIVING ROOM PHARMACY

There are those occasions when a good business deserves a better identity.

The Modern Family Pharmacy in Vancouver had established a loyal—and well-heeled—customer base with its focus on family, a stylish product selection (personal care products from Provence) and a free coffee bar where customers can wait on their prescriptions. When the owner of the "boutique pharmacy" approached Spring for a new logo, the rationale was that the success of the business called for a more professional mark than the home-built identity it had started with. But at step 2, Spring turned up a very different—and more urgent—concern.

The market study found that while customers enjoyed their interactions with the pharmacy, its name provoked little or no recognition. "The existing customer base referred to the business by the owner's name, all sorts of things—but not Modern Family Pharmacy," notes Chua. "We knew there was a problem with the name and

not with the business itself." But challenging the customer right off the bat wasn't the smart way to proceed, Chua reasoned. Instead, the agency went ahead with its four-step process.

"If we'd said in the first meeting with the client, 'You're going to have to change your name because it's terrible,' the relationship wouldn't have gone too far. Instead, we talked about why they came to us in the first place." These discussions, backed up with a brand study on the client, became the basis for a solution that was a radical departure from the store's previous logo, but far closer to the true nature of the business.

Your Name Again? Sometimes, the problem isn't the logo; it's the name. When research demonstrated this boutique pharmacy's name suggested anything but the personalized service that made it successful, the owners agreed more than a new logo was needed—a new name was, too. Spring sprung into action.
(Before: top, After: bottom)

In unveiling the new name and visual personality to the client, Spring's strategy was to focus on customer experience. "We told the client we were going to retain all the positive brand attributes like the family focus and comfort," Chua says. "We had to tell them, 'Your name right now isn't doing that—it's all the other things you do. Your name is generic, but how you're operating your business isn't.' The new logo and identity needed to feel safe, comforting, and somehow familiar."

An apt example of capturing visual personality, the new logo is based on what Chua calls a "hug and a pestle." Two open hands meet to form a bowl, and with the grinding stick, the pestle, together they're the recognized symbol for a pharmacy. A subtle *Rx* was also incorporated into the *Living Room* wordmark. The result is an identity that looks right, feels comfortable— and like the business itself—insists on being remembered.

ARTICULATE THE PERSONALITY
FFUN MOTOR GROUP

When Spring took on the job of redesigning the visual personality of the FFun Motor Group, they knew that the brand had a good starting point. "There was equity in the previous logo," Chua says. "People identified with the double-arrow symbol. It made some people think of speed; some saw a 'fast forward' symbol, which was part of the intent behind the original design."

>>
FFun
Motor Group

Vrrrooom. "Fast forward" is a fine association for a business that deals with automobiles and speed. The double arrows in this company's logo had equity worth keeping, so Vancouver-based Spring made them a prominent feature in the company's new identity.
(Before: top, After: bottom)

Spring decided to keep the double-arrow, but they reframed it, creating a fresher, more contemporary design, especially through typography. The new type is, in Chua's words, "less Swiss," with softer edges and less-structured letterforms to create a more approachable feel than the previous Helvetica. The addition of the rounded box gives the logo a stronger visual presence, something the original logo was lacking.

Because the motor group operates auto dealerships, having a flexible and friendly visual personality is a critical attribute. Car buyers look for fast response, clear answers (such as quotes) and a personal touch. Elements from the new Motor Group logo now appear as graphical touches within the dealerships, sending the message that doing business with the dealer will indeed be "fast and fun." "For instance, the group created a guarantee that the dealer will give a prospective buyer a quote within fifteen minutes or the customer gets a free oil change," says Chua. Dependable, speedy, generous service: just what the new graphics, with a combination of sleekness and warmth, lead a customer to expect.

More evidence that smart logo redesigns never occur in a vacuum, and that the intricate links between image and execution—and between the customer's emotional investment and the client's business model—must always be respected.

DEVELOP THE IDENTITY.
THE SHRUNKS

It's a good name for a punk band, but The Shrunks is actually a line of products intended to help youngsters address common bedtime fears: fear of the dark, monsters in the closet—all of the anxieties that can make going to bed a harrowing ordeal for children (and the parents they keep awake).

Conceived and located in Vancouver, The Shrunks products include toys, gadgets, plush dolls (including hapless little monsters who are scared of you) and inflatable beds. They're personified in The Shrunks' Family, a family of four (plus "Sunny, the Fearless Guard Dog") whose defining physical feature is that they always keep one eye open to stay on guard against things that go bump in the night. The description of Sunny gets the idea across:

"Sunny, the Fearless Guard Dog, will help make fear disappear. Specially trained by The Shrunks, he sleeps with one eye open and one eye closed, so he can watch over you when you are sleeping."

The Shrunks' parent company approached Spring about redesigning

Cute, Cuter, Cutest. What's keeping you up at night? Maybe it pays to play to customer fears, but a more positive approach has its merits. The Shrunks are children's products that dispel fears. Spring gave the brand's puppy watchdog a sweet, rounder visage. Good boy.
(Before: above left, After: above)

the line's logo when feedback from customers and retail sales experts indicated a retune was in order. The research suggested that instead of saying "We'll help you fight your fears," the message should be about building confidence and creating fun bedtime rituals.

"The target market tends to gravitate toward brands that have friendly personalities and especially faces," Chua said. The original logo, which, incidentally, Spring had designed, "needed to be reworked to include this component, and the dog character from The Shrunks' Family seemed the obvious choice."

Articulating the personality of The Shrunks products—step 3 in Spring's process—brought up descriptors like *playful, funky, lively, clean, simple, cute.* Spring's team investigated similar brands that also possessed these characteristics. "The former logo was an abstract representation of a watchful

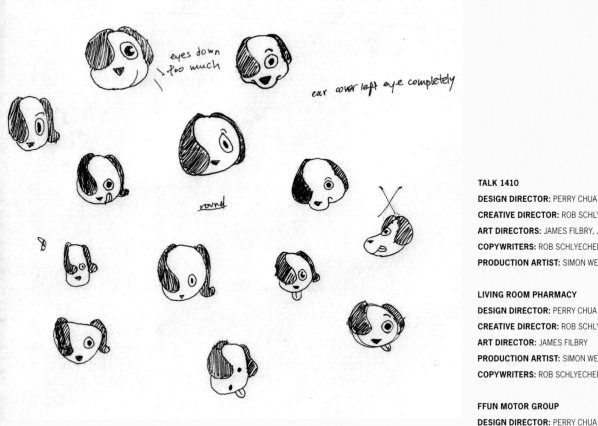

- rounder face
- cuter face

eyes down too much

ear cover left eye completely

round

eye," Chua notes. "The target market resonates more with a literal icon, something with a face and expressive features. A face is easier for a child to identify with, and a puppy has an association with reliability and protection."

The new "Sunny-based" logo is more in keeping with the spirit of the overall brand. Yet a closer look at the underlying elements of the before and after logos reveals there were graphical elements retained in the transition—the comforting circular forms and the single watchful eye among them. Also retained was the type style of The Shrunks wordmark.

Overall, while the emotional resonance of The Shrunks identity persists, the message is now more positive. Instead of focusing on fighting fear, the identity now addresses confidence building. "Is one better than the other?" Chua asks. "Not necessarily. The strategy and the goals are different now, and we're adjusting our approach to meet the market."

TALK 1410
DESIGN DIRECTOR: PERRY CHUA
CREATIVE DIRECTOR: ROB SCHLYECHER
ART DIRECTORS: JAMES FILBRY, JEREMY GRICE
COPYWRITERS: ROB SCHLYECHER, JESSICA MORI
PRODUCTION ARTIST: SIMON WEST

LIVING ROOM PHARMACY
DESIGN DIRECTOR: PERRY CHUA
CREATIVE DIRECTOR: ROB SCHLYECHER
ART DIRECTOR: JAMES FILBRY
PRODUCTION ARTIST: SIMON WEST
COPYWRITERS: ROB SCHLYECHER, JESSICA MORI

FFUN MOTOR GROUP
DESIGN DIRECTOR: PERRY CHUA
CREATIVE DIRECTOR: ROB SCHLYECHER
ART DIRECTOR: JAMES FILBRY
PRODUCT ARTIST: SIMON WEST
COPYWRITERS: ROB SCHLYECHER, JESSICA MORI

THE SHRUNKS
DESIGN DIRECTOR: PERRY CHUA
DESIGNERS: SHON TANNER, GEORGE LIN
PRODUCTION ARTIST: SHON TANNER

GLOSSARY

The glossary of terms listed below will be referenced often throughout this book.

LOGO, MARK, SYMBOL

—a graphic that wholly stands for the company or its product; it may or may not have the logotype within it

COLOR PALETTE

—a color system that is specific to the company or its products

BRAND

—like identity, the sum of all visual elements that characterize a company or its product

LOGOTYPE

—a lettering system designed specifically for a company or its product; it can be freestanding or stand beside the logo

IDENTITY

—the sum of all visual elements

BRANDING

—the art and science of constructing brand personality

ABCDEFGHIJKLM
NOPQRSTUVWXYZ
0123456789

FONT

—all letter families

IDENTITY SYSTEM

—the strategically based order of how that identity gets visually represented in any way

VISUAL PERSONALITY

—coined by Ph.D, the visual representation of the qualities, characteristics, and soul of a company or product

Brian Collins

A Logo Supreme

DESIGN: COLLINS:
NEW YORK

MEDIA ARE EXPLODING. Platforms are multiplying. New systems of communication, like weeds, are constantly sprouting up and tangling, turning each other into compost. The world of brand design, says Brian Collins, is moving, and "the challenge for designers is to move dynamically along with the world."

For Collins, whose eponymous firm works with some of the best-known brands, the potential impediments to such dynamic movement are many. One risk is that in the attempt to keep up with messy new media, a designer may end up just adding to the mess:

"As media get more complex, we have to create systems people can navigate through more simply," Collins says. "Otherwise they'll become paralyzed by the tidal waves of information hitting them. What good identity can do is to bring clarity and understanding to that confusion."

There's also the risk of getting bogged down by old ideas—such as the traditional faith that the logo is supreme. Collins, who admits that he still swoons for a good mark—"They're something we, as artists, love to make, a synthesis of ideas crystallized into one image"—believes nevertheless that "a logo is not as important as its system. The system is far more central today than it's ever been. You might be saddled with a lousy logo, but if you have a really smart system to give it clarity, it can still be effective."

In today's media environment, an excessive concern with logo design can amount to distraction, even laziness.

Lousy Logos Redeemed. Collins believes that a lousy mark can be overcome with a good identity system. What makes a system good? Consistency, logic, clarity, and functionality. "The real work and the real intelligence," he says, "is giving that identity life."

"My concern is that we still are obsessed with the craft of making the logo itself, without realizing that the real craft, the real work and the real intelligence—is in giving that identity life, so it moves energetically across communications and environments and products," Collins says. "That's the work. The real craft is the system, not the object."

INSTANT STORYTELLING

"Having conversations about 'How much I hate or love that logo' can be cathartic for designers, but they're ultimately academic," Collins says. "For most people, it's moot because they experience identity dynamically—when they buy a product, when they go into a store, when they see it online, when they're playing a game, or downloading a mobile application. That's where identities Live."

His firm's "we" mark for Al Gore's Alliance for Climate Protection is carefully designed for life in multiple applications. Collins says, "Here's a visual idea that not only needed to work across communications, products, and environments but across widely different political platforms as well. It has to be a call to action and live everywhere, boldly. So we made it as simple—and blunt—as possible."

The toughest challenge, for Collins, was that the logo had to be more than an image. It had to be a story. "This can be hard to do," Collins says. "Most logos aren't that successful when they have a ready-made narrative baked in. Logos are usually better as vessels—you fill in the meaning based on your own experiences." The solution presents the word "we" inside a warm green circle, with an upside-down *m* serving for the *w*. A story in an image: *me* becomes *we*. It's difficult to imagine a two-letter statement the ethos of environmentalism more complete than that.

"Instant storytelling," Collins calls it. If he's right, we'll be seeing more of the technique. "In brand messages, I believe we'll be moving into an era not unlike the last great technological shifts—back in the early 1900s, when electricity, airplanes, radio, and television appeared. Take a look at brands then, like Morton Salt—'When it rains it pours.' A girl walks underneath a giant

Old Dog, New Tricks. Even the most famous names and wordmarks can stand a little trip to the powder room on occasion. Over the decades, Kodak has adapted its wordmark to signal that it remains an innovative leader in photographic technology. Consider the equity Kodak has in yellow and red in a box. Does it still look like a box of Kodachrome to you?
(Before: below, After: above)

1935

1960

1971

1987

1987

1987

umbrella. Maxwell House comes from the same era—'Good to the last drop.' accompanied by a coffee cup tipped with the final drop coming out. These instant stories were so memorable that they retain their impact generations later," he notes.

THE POWER OF CONTEXT

Creativity often manifests itself in a certain relish for provocation, and Collins enjoys spelling out the more radical conclusions of his context-based design philosophy. Regarding a certain swoosh, Collins declares, "The Nike logo could be any shape."

Yes, even that legendary mark "is powerful because of the company's brilliant products, and marketing—as well as its association with the best athletes of our time," Collins says. "Until it's surrounded by communication that connects it to Al Gore's mission, or seen in the TV commercials done with the Martin Agency, you really don't understand what the logo is inviting you to do—what action to take. The logo can sometimes carry the meaning alone, but to work best, is has to live within a strong story."

For Collins, logo-worship is an outdated superstition. "All kinds of companies have tried to do something that looks like Nike's logo. It's sad to see the swooshification of brands. When companies say, 'We want something that looks contemporary like Nike,' it's magical thinking," he says. "They're trying to use a logo like a talisman. The talisman isn't the power; the power is the people who hold it and know how to use it."

Product Is King. The power of any logo is the sum of many parts. Kodak's iconic image is a sum of its brilliant products, marketing, and advertising over generations. Until a mark is surrounded by communication, Collins reminds us, it has little value or meaning.

WE
DESIGN DIRECTOR: BRIAN COLLINS
CREATIVE DIRECTOR: SEAN RILEY
ART DIRECTOR: TY HARPER
DESIGNERS: JOHN MOON, MICKEY PANGILINAN
COPYWRITER: RAYMOND MCKINNEY
TYPOGRAPHY: CHESTER JENKINS, VILLAGE

KODAK
CREATIVE DIRECTOR: BRIAN COLLINS
DESIGN DIRECTOR: ALLEN HORI
DESIGNER: CHRISTIAN CERVANTES

MID-CENTURY MOTOROLA

"I love the logo Morton Goldsholl designed for Motorola in the 1950s," Collins says. "It's a brilliant piece of Mid-Century Modern graphics. Few people really appreciate how profound his influence was in American design."

Yet Motorola was about to abandon its logo in the late '90s. A new identity had been designed, and Collins was called in for consultation before it was launched. "I had to be honest," he recalls. "I suggested the reason their current logo looked dated was not because it was old, but because their technology and design of their phones looked so dated. It wasn't the logo. It was its context. Their clunky cell phones had not been redesigned in over three years. Worse, they looked like they had been designed for trench warfare."

Motorola's competitors—Nokia, Samsung, LG, Ericsson—were introducing more stylish, slick phones. "The engineers at Motorola are better than anyone, but they were behind the curve in understanding how design now had badge value. A phone expressed yourself like a watch, jewelry, or fashion," Collins says. Fortunately, Motorola had more exciting designs in the pipeline. Collins asked Motorola to keep its old logo, but with minor alterations meant especially for placement on the upcoming, new phones and digital technologies.

"I pleaded with them to keep the logo—but to just reverse it, and do it in only thirty-six bold colors. We tweaked the *M*, made the mark a little sharper, so when it went down really small on a mobile device you would be able to read it easily. I said, 'If you do this, one thing, you won't have to spend millions of dollars changing everything. Keep your sign on your manufacturing plant in China. Keep your corporate stationery in Chicago. All you have to do

M Is For Mid-Century. "We seem to be a constant rebirth of Mid-Century Modernism right now," says Brian Collins, "and I loved the smart design that embodied the boundless enthusiasm of postwar America."

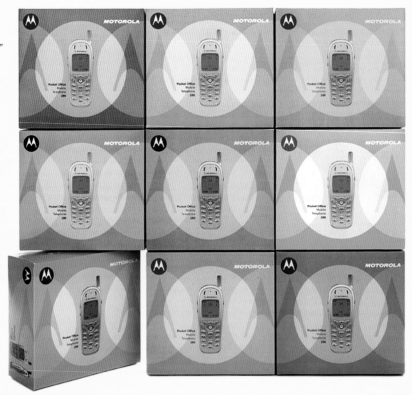

at first is change the advertising and your packaging and branding on your products—all of which you're going to do anyway.'

"The second thing I suggested was this: 'If you stick with this *M* symbol alone—and are disciplined about managing it—in five years you won't have to use the Motorola name on your packaging or products at all. The *M* will be instantly recognized, globally.' They made it in three years." The revitalized identity was part of the company's rebirth, and Collins is proud his team helped preserve the company's design legacy.

"We seem to be in a constant rebirth of Mid-Century Modernism right now," he says. "And I loved smart design that embodied the boundless enthusiasm of postwar America."

Collins concludes, "We can't just abandon this kind of great work to museums and design history books, especially when it still works so well today. With Motorola, we fought to show how it could be made better than ever."

MOTOROLA
AGENCY: BRAND INTEGRATION GROUP/OGILVY
EXECUTIVE CREATIVE DIRECTOR: BRIAN COLLINS
CREATIVE DIRECTOR: MICHAEL KAYE
DESIGN DIRECTORS: ALAN DYE, THOMAS VASQUEZ
DESIGNERS: MAJA BLAZEJEWSKA, STELLA BUGBEE, EDWARD CHIQUITUCTO, JASON RING

CHAPTER 2

The Only Constant: Change

WHEN IT COMES TO THE EVOLUTION of brands, there is no better example than the soft drink industry to demonstrate that in order to survive, successful brands have to adapt or die. The evolution of brands' logos or logotypes is often for strategic purposes, rather than change just for the sake of change. Typically, the reason is simple, but the causes are varied:

- The brand is not connecting with the intended audience
- Its message is muddled, confusing
- Its message is outdated or no longer relevant
- Its message is reaching an unintended audience
- Its message is reaching an established audience but one in decline; to grow, the brand needs a newer or younger audience

Carb-Counting Colonel. In the '50s, '60s, and '70s who knew that polyunsaturated fat would lead to heart disease? Fast-food famous brands that don't adapt changing social tastes and mores are doomed. Even the once chunky Colonel looks like he's been munching more grilled than fried poultry these days. Are those really his cheekbones?

As mentioned in Chapter One, what many call "visual identity" or "the brand," I call *visual personality*. It is easier to think of a product or company visually if you think of it as a person. We share memories with them, fond ones mostly, but sometimes the person you loved changes. He or she is no longer the person you knew. You hardly recognize them. Or, conversely, you've changed but they have not. You no longer find them useful or meaningful.

For brands, gaps between past and present perception can alienate existing customers and keep new customers from giving you a try. If people no longer understand you, you will not attract them as buyers, customers, partners, employees, vendors, or suppliers. The way you redesign your brand's visual personality can help you to close the gaps between perception and reality and, thus, preserve your brand's life.

NEW MENU ITEMS

Consider some famous restaurant brands that once served only products such as super-sized meals loaded with polyunsaturated fat and salt. Few cared about such things in the 1960s and '70s, but studies and awareness caused a slow evolution of consumer thinking about health and nutrition. Today, any fast-food company that does not offer healthier choices would be pilloried by public opinion.

ARE YOU UNTHINKING WHAT I'M UNTHINKING?

TASTE THE UNFRIED SIDE OF KFC.

www.unthinkfc.com

In fact, big restaurant corporations spend millions trying to stay ahead of the curve—and ahead of the perception that they are the principle cause of obesity among young people. They measure consumer tastes, develop and test products in order to satisfy those tastes. Once tested and proven, these food empires spend billions more on operational improvements in order to get fresher offerings onto serving trays or into compostable to-go containers. You have to give them full marks for trying. But are people always aware that these changes have been made?

Not really. If public opinion still perceives you as serving food that kills, the billions invested in real change is money wasted.

You can't just make changes. You must *communicate* them. You must tell people. You must get their attention and make certain that the changes are perceived. Otherwise, those lovely new broiled chicken wraps and meatless burritos will find no hungry customer. What is more, you get no credit for your sensitivity to the tastes of health-conscious moms and fat-free scolds.

OUR HERO: YOU

Who can save Burger House from a hostile, more healthful world? You, the visual personality adjuster, the brand consultant, the identity expert, the designer at the international branding firm or you, there, working from your garage studio. No one is better qualified than you to identify the gaps between perception and reality, measure them, and then develop creative (and effective) solutions to close them.

Visual personality makeovers, or rebranding, should be performed only in the face of chasms between perception and reality. "I am a respectable green business. Consumers see me as a callous polluter of creeks beside daycare centers. How can I make them change their minds?" Here's how:

- Find the gaps through careful assessment.
- Close these gaps through creative solutions based upon that assessment.
- Let them know the value of your solutions.

BRAIN SURGERY OR GARDENING?

You cannot solve a visual personality disorder unless you understand the roots of the problem. What caused a brand to get out of whack? Why are audiences not connecting with the brand? You've got to dig and find out. And the more time you're spending rooting out the causes of disconnect and wrong signals, the better informed you will be when you begin the time-consuming and deliciously painful process of developing your certain award-winning solution.

Different design concerns call it different things. Some call it brand discovery or brand assessment—some even have pretentiously branded the company due-diligence process with serious sounding names as though it were brain surgery. It isn't. It's more like gardening: The better you clear the patch, prepare the soil, and plant the seeds, the better the broccoli come summer.

Little Black Box. When Saks Fifth Avenue approached Pentagram to design a new identity, partner Michael Bierut, and his team quickly realized that this was more than a logo design project. The history of Saks showed that they had used dozens of logos since their founding. Many of these were variations on a theme: cursive writing,

THREE STEPS TO SUCCESS

Assessment involves three basic tactical steps: the visual audit, the competitive audits, and interviews with stakeholder audiences. The process for assessment might be more in depth at a bigger branding agency working for a large corporate client, than the local clients of a small design office.

SNIFFING LOW AND SUCKING UP

Sure, there are differences between how the Big Chaps Agency and the Small Blokes Studio tackle a rebranding project. They are evidenced throughout this book. Generally speaking, the complexity of a case and the size of a client dictate the budget and the depth of research you conduct.

Big corporate makeovers involve big corporate turf wars and politics. You think the senior brand managers at Intuit's QuickBooks brand wanted any change to their brand identity? Well, not without some serious face time to get their input and buy in. (See page 58 for details on the Intuit brand story.)

1940

1946

1955

1955

1973

1997

2007

sometimes casual script, sometimes Spencerian. Bierut took the 1973 version of the logo as his foundation, redrew it with font designer Joe Finocchiaro, and enclosed it in a black box to create a classic logo.

To make change, you have to cultivate consensus among management, employees, and resellers and, through traditional or non traditional focus groups, among consumers. In essence, to reach your goal of a new logo and identity system, you have to let a lot of stakeholder doggies sniff your leg and pee on your well-made shoes. You must encourage participation and make them part of the solution. And sometimes you can make them think that *they came up with the solution*!

Modest clients with rebranding needs may have less to invest in discovery, but discover they must. Remember, even if the depth of your client's pockets is limited, your thirst for knowledge is not. The more you know about the causes of the perception problem, the more on the mark your proposed solutions will be. Likewise, the more buy in you get from internal and external stakeholders, the less push back you get when you begin presenting plausible solutions that otherwise would have been considered crazy.

> "Visual personality makeovers, or rebranding, should be performed only in the face of chasms between perception and reality."

You can never learn *too* much. Therefore, take the time to assess the problem before you begin trying to solve it. The next step is to start applying that knowledge.

Visual assessment can be simple or complex. Generally speaking, the bigger the company, the more stuff it has to stick its logo on. So when trying to discover the causes of perception gaps, sometimes you have to spend a lot of time going through the company's attic and basement reviewing what has and has not worked well in the past.

EQUITY: VALUE IS RELATIVE

The equity of a brand is its value. A brand can have positive equity or negative equity and, in either case, it is accumulated over time. Equity is a historical fact with contemporary implications. Therefore, the goal of *anyone* charged with the task of moving a brand's visual personality *forward* is about proper assessment and assignment of brand equity.

What elements of that personality—the brand's story—should be carried forward? What elements should be dumped in the river? Be careful. For the most part, anything with positive connotation warrants keeping: The shape of the bottle, the color of that famous delivery truck, that swoosh on my shoe, or that script on my baby powder. These elements are tangible, not perceived, but they bring to mind intangible associations of *past* experiences. Some imply continuity and stability. Some suggest fun times or warm family moments, and so on.

But how do you invest your valuable brand equity? Do we lock it in the family vault? Or do we let it roam freely in bright green (sustainable) meadows, under the clear (smog-free) blue skies, free and happy? That depends upon whom you ask.

Puma, a manufacturer of apparel and footwear, retains most of its equity in its iconic sleek, leaping cat. But this company allows designers to be "promiscuous" with that cat, emblazoning it on shoes, apparel, and accessories in all manner and derivations with one recent ad featuring half man, half cat—an erotic Puma representation.

Don't count on Coke putting its contour curve on a naked woman anytime soon. Coke, on the other hand, is more circumspect. It boils its brand equity down to four basic elements:

- The contour (of the bottle)
- The wave, also known as the dynamic ribbon (graphic)
- The script (signature)
- The color red

LIGHT INJECTED FOOTWEAR

To much extent, design providers have been given permission to be creative and playful in the vast universe beyond those elements. But no one—but God—can mess with those four elements. Now, think about that: an enormous brand with worldwide audiences boils its vast brand equity down to four simple elements. That is smart.

Be smart: One brand's positive is another brand's death sentence. "Continuity," for instance, is good if you are a bank, bad if you make snowboard gear. "Safe" is a great if you make baby formula but a drag if your company sells fresh ideas. "Positive" is relative. When assessing a brand's equity you have to determine not only who or what a brand was and is, but who or what that brand hopes to be.

Honor the past. Face reality. Design for the future. But above all else, change.

Bolt Upright. David Turner, a fan of the rebranding of Puma says, "In the '90s they [Puma] decided that they were no longer a sports equipment brand but rather a sport lifestyle brand. They've embraced style and fashion in really interesting ways. They allow their leaping puma cat to be desecrated in some ways and yet somehow retain its integrity."

8.5 FL OZ (250 mL)

David Turner

A Nice Turner Round

Q: OK, first things first: Thank you for making my mother's pantry look so nice. Your lovely work for Waitrose supermarkets in England has enhanced her health and her décor. Now, I read an article recently where you talked about how important wit was to you. At Ph.D, we always try to integrate wit into our work. It's great to put a smile on someone's face.

DT: When a Belgian magazine interviewed me not long ago, I discovered that there isn't a Flemish word for *wit*. It turns out the word is missing in many languages. It's an English word. Working here in the States, I find it fascinating that what many Americans most value about British design is wit.

Q: The drier the better, so far as I can tell. Let's talk about your work for Coca-Cola. I am a lifelong fan. I started collecting Coke bottles from other countries when I was a young lad. Your move to take the Coke brand back to its simplest element—the color, the wave, and the script—was so clever. (Is there a Belgium word for *clever*, by the way?) Did the idea go over well when first presented?

DT: I recently looked back at our first presentation of the simplification concept, and it looks pretty much exactly like what it came to be. When we showed the idea to their Creative Excellence Group, they got it, it was exactly what they wanted. But it was a long, hard sell to get other stakeholders with Coke to accept it. To be honest, the only reason it all happened was the Creative Excellence Group—especially Pio Schunker, Moira Cullen, and Frederick Kahn—were relentless.

Q: What was the brief?

DT: We had been doing other bits for Coke, new brand stuff and reinterpretations of old brands—R&D, basically. Pio Schunker said he wanted us to work on the red brand. Hugely flattering, of course, though I wasn't the collector you were, because there's something about Coca-Cola branding and design. My business partner calls it the "Mount Everest" brand—the pinnacle.

Q: Consider the long history of greats who have touched that brand, J. C. Leyendecker, Norman Rockwell … all those wonderful old ads. All that wonderful, collectable "stuff."

DT: Precisely. A great, rich heritage. But I had concerns. Our creative reputation is more important to us than anything. I was afraid the sheer scale of the brand could consume us. I could see ourselves two years down the road with little great work to show for it and burned out to boot. I was concerned that it wouldn't be the best cultural fit.

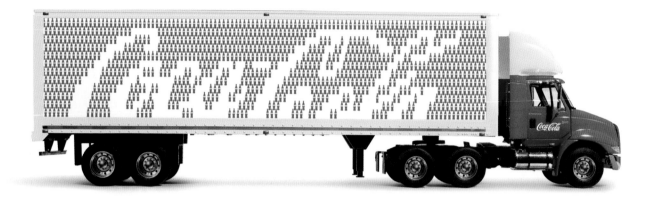

But Pio told me that was why he was hiring us: he wanted an independent agency willing to fight for great creative. Reviewing recent advertising, I saw some very simple ads that had this great little sign off, "It's nice to have a Coke." And I thought, okay, they're finally getting it again. This really encouraged me.

Q: Your Coca-Cola brand story is the epitome of this book's thesis: discerning the equity and leveraging in a rebranding scheme. Talk to us, please, in those terms. How did you decide what element to keep and which to set aside?
DT: Let's say we were talking about a new brand, something you aren't familiar with. Or you might think you know what the equity is because it is predominant, like the color blue, for instance. Not so with Coke: we had a strong opinion on what equities were important. And that was reason we got to simplify it. The can, for instance, had all the key elements: the Spenserian Coca-Cola script, the dynamic ribbon, and Coke red. (It did not have another critical design element with vast equity: the contour of the bottle.) But it also was layered with different reds, touches of yellow, graphic bubbles, and water drops.

Many at the time thought all that other stuff had equity. We told them those other bits and pieces were diluting the brand's most critical equities. And because we talked equity, our ideas carried weight. We weren't perceived as just some designers who advocated change for change's sake. We convinced them that bubbles were generic to the category; it's not specific to Coke, it cannot hold equity. It was a great way to get the client to simplify and focus. There are very few things that are truly unique to that brand.

Q: But you didn't go back to the original look, right?

DT: Right. We did not want to go backwards. We wanted to use the past to help remind the audience what made Coke great. We wanted to take those things and make them modern and fresh. I think the reason the branding scheme has garnered so much attention is that we pulled off a neat trick: people see it and say to themselves, "Wow, this really is the Coke that I knew and loved." Well it is—and isn't: it's contemporary and new. I'm not quite sure how we pulled that off, but I am grateful we did.

It's amazing how so many people have a happy nostalgic association with the brand. There is something kind of magical about it, and that magic has been part of our culture for years. It's a great brand, and we're having so much fun working on it.

Q: So you were able to convince them that these key elements are your core assets and they are so strong that you don't need any others. And then you applied those assets to new ideas such as the aluminum bottle.

DT: Yes, contemporary ideas we could bring them using the same elements in a fresh way.

Q: On your website, you talk about a framework that values intuition and perception as highly as metrics. Can you talk about that?

DT: Long ago, my partner and I used to work at the same agency and there was a very smart, down-to-earth woman who worked in the financial department. She didn't know a thing about design but you'd always take your design to her. We called it the "Marion test." We'd say "Did it pass the Marion test?" She was an ordinary person who didn't pull any punches

Ubiquitous. Everything this book needed to know, it learned from Coca-Cola: Distill a brand's equity to it's most fundamental—unique—elements and then put them to use in fresh, contemporary, and compelling ways. Coke's style is a velvet sledgehammer.

and told you the facts. Designers are prone to kidding themselves—we've got some brilliant ideas that we can't let go of and Marion would be the reality check. Our panel testing is based on the Marion test: it is a quick reality check with the right kind of consumer who helps us make sure we're not wasting time. We will interview consumers one by one, record, and then play the feedback to the designer working on the project that day at her desk. These consumers talk about the things that the designer just did, which means by the end of the day he or she could have altered and improved their design.

Q: Can you name a few other redesigns that have impressed you?

DT: I'm keen on the rebranding of Puma. Back in the '90s they decided that they were no longer a sports equipment brand but, rather, a sport lifestyle brand. So they embraced style and fashion in really interesting ways. They allow their leaping puma cat to be desecrated in some ways and yet somehow retain its integrity. They're creating a vibrant, youthful, exciting identity. Things like Alexander McQueen's version of their logo that's a photograph by Nick Knight that's half human/half puma and super sexy. Of course they have, like Nike, Apple, or any big retail brand, the advantage of constantly changing repertoire of products. A challenge with Coke is that it's the same product it's always been—and it's not going to change. You don't have a new high-tech version of Coke coming out to keep it interesting. Only the visual identity can do that. Another example I talk about from the fashion area is Burberry. I was speaking with one of the owners of the company one day, and he told me that it all started when they hired Kate Moss and put her in an ad wearing a bikini made out of their fabric. The intention was to make their raincoats a bit sexier, but what happened was the company got inundated with requests for a Burberry bikini. They were on to something. But you think about it a moment: a Burberry raincoat was a middle-aged English man's boring way of keeping the rain off his dull blue suit. It was a dull, stodgy, traditional pattern that was not cool at all. But then some smart branding people decided to work with this dull pattern—to push it as far as they could in every direction and make it cool. They realized their pattern was the biggest logo in the fashion industry—a logo people could wear all over their body. They were willing to play with it and not treat it with too much reverence or restriction. A modern brand identity has to be open, flexible, and adaptive. It has to interact with its environment. The more you let it adapt and change within its environment, the more exciting it is. The old approach is to apply the logo exactly the same size in precisely the same place on everything. This is what we call a gas station approach to branding that is outdated.

Q: So, do you drink Coca-Cola?
DT: I drink Coke Zero because I'm diabetic. I certainly drank Coke before that, but my whole day of carbohydrates in one can, I can't do. But my kids drink it. These drinks are getting a little bit of a bad rap these days, unfairly; I mean it's always had sugar in it, so it's all about quantity and how you fit it in to your lifestyle. I used to only have Coke when I was a kid when I was on holiday; so I always associate that taste with being on holiday, so it always gives me a good feeling.

Q: I had an uncle in Cyprus, and I went to visit him one summer. It was very hot there, very hot, and I drank Coke all the time. That's my biggest Coca-Cola memory. Nowadays, I really don't like it, it's too sweet for my taste. But, every now and then, I have to have a sip to remind myself of Cyprus when I was drinking it all the time with lots of ice and lemon.

DT: It's amazing how so many and have a happy nostalgic association with the brand, even you and you don't even drink the stuff. There is something kind of magical about it and that magic has been part of our culture for years. It's a great brand and we're having so much fun working on it.

CREATIVE DIRECTORS: DAVID TURNER AND BRUCE DUCKWORTH
COCA-COLA ALUMINUM BOTTLE
DESIGNER: CHRIS GARVEY
COCA-COLA TRUCKS
DESIGN DIRECTOR: SARAH MOFFAT
DESIGNERS: JONATHAN WARNER, RADU RANGA, JOSH MICHELS, REBECCA WILLIAMS, CHRIS GARVEY
COCA-COLA TRANSPARENT CUP
DESIGN DIRECTOR: SARAH MOFFAT
DESIGNERS: CHRIS GARVEY, JOSH MICHELS

Sleight of Hand (Evolution)

REFRESHING

SOMETIMES, THE ONLY THING A BRAND NEEDS IS A LITTLE REFRESHING. Perhaps the type is off or the color palette appears dated. Whatever the case, the change to the logo or identity system can be subtle or dramatic, but the visual personality of the brand remains largely intact.

One thing that should never be encouraged is change for the sake of change. There has to be a compelling reason to revisit a brand's logo, its primary visual asset. All of that is information that will be discovered in the research and brand equity assessment at the outset of the project.

Since we have covered the subject of equity assessment in the previous chapter, let us turn our attention to specific cases in this book that fall into the category of evolutionary rather than revolutionary change.

MUCH-NEEDED CHANGE

Perhaps one of the finest examples of this is the updated Delta Airlines brand by Lippincott, New York. Then again, rebranding programs for any airline are dramatic, whether the change is revolutionary or evolutionary. The reason for this is simple: enormity. Just imagine the cost of repainting all the vehicles required of an airline, from the planes to the baggage service vehicles. The slightest tweak to an existing logo could cost millions.

Delta's updated identity was launched simultaneous with its emergence from Chapter 11. This was a strategic decision. The rationale behind the change was to inform employees and customers that this is a new Delta under new management—it's financially stronger, better managed and at peace with its employees.

According to Lippincott designer Brendán Murphy, "There was much negative sentiment toward the people who had taken the company into Chapter 11. They wanted to signal change internally and externally. They want to force reconsideration of the brand on audiences inside and outside the company. To arrive at the solution, we had to meet with both management and employees every time we visited them in Atlanta to ensure that management was taking employees into consideration every step of the way."

Still, in the case of Delta, great change was signaled in subtle ways. First and foremost, according to Connie Birdsall at Lippincott, no one wanted to get rid of the Delta "widget," the fourth letter of the Greek alphabet used in mathemathics to signal change.

There was huge, huge heritage in what Delta staff affectionately call the Delta widget, especially among employees whose opinions and input were to be vital to the success of the company. In my entire career, I've never worked on a project where the emotion around a symbol and the history of the company was so strong."

The result was a fresh, simplified look that signaled change that reflects both the brand's heritage (the widget remains) but definitely an airline moving ahead. "We definitely went back and looked at the historical typography. This final is a more modern rendition. We had some renditions of the design that were incredibly retro looking, but in the end we wanted something that, while it had a link to the past, was really more clean and modern and more for the future," Birdsall notes.

"That program was all about making it clean and simple and professional-looking. Something that could last a long time and wasn't fussy," adds Murphy, who also worked on the project.

Airline identity changes involve changes on thousands of vehicles and equipment at enormous cost. Given the client was emerging from Chapter 11, the Lippincott team was very mindful of this when it was time to execute the design. "We didn't want to create a design that was going to cost more to implement than what they already had. The flowing fabric design

Ready When You Are. Chapter 11 ain't all that bad. Delta emerged from it a leaner and more competitive company. Management and employees wanted to signal that change to its customers without destroying the valuable equity it had in its name and its famous "widget." (Before: top, After: bottom)

DELTA

CREATIVE DIRECTOR: CONNIE BIRDSALL
ART DIRECTORS: ADAM STRINGER, FABIAN DIAZ
DESIGNERS: ADAM STRINGER, FABIAN DIAZ, KEVIN HAMMOND, MICHAEL MILLIGAN
PRODUCTION: BRENDAN DEVALLANCE, JEREMY DARTY

had something like six or seven paint masks for the tail. I think it took well over a week to paint one plane with that tail," explains Murphy. "The new paint job takes only three days. They only make money when the planes are up in the air. So anything you can do to reduce the weight of plane and the time it takes to paint positively effects the bottom line."

The Delta case study demonstrates an important point: no matter how angry many Delta employees had been at the senior managers who dragged them and their reputation into bankruptcy in order to reorganize, they still loved the heritage of their brand. New management at Delta clearly understood this and retained the most symbolic Delta identifier: the delta. Out went the complex—and expensive to reproduce and paint—flag-styled tail graphic created during the Atlanta 1996 Summer Olympic Games. The font was simplified. The red, white, and blue logo and logotype became just red and white.

CENTER STAGE

The brand identities for the Brooklyn Botanical Garden and the Hartford Stage (see case studies pages 100 and 114) designed by Carbone Smolan, New York, are equally fine examples of a light hand that clarifies and rejuvenates a brand. At a glance, these before and after images might appear quite different. But the central concepts behind both identities remain in place. Older audiences will notice something new, yet take comfort in the familiar—but new audiences and young supporters of both of these civic arts and cultural institutions hopefully will see the old garden and stage in a completely new light. That is where design can be magic.

The old Hartford logo simply did not convey the energy of this highly respected arts organization that had won a coveted Tony Award for Outstanding Regional Theater in America. With that recognition, the theater directors saw great potential in reaching out to new audiences beyond their hometown in big cities such as nearby New York and Boston. The Carbone Smolan solution was based upon the concept of a "Colorful

Cast of Characters" and while quite different from the older, duller version, still retains its sense of humility and restraint without being dull and unsophisticated.

The Brooklyn Botanic Garden's previous logo was dated and congested. It had an Art Deco air about it. The new identity retains the equity of the botanical concept but replaces congestion with tranquility—it cut through the vines and weeds and left the identity with a well-maintained garden. The graphic plant form can now be separated from the logotype so as to be used in all manner of application from signage and banners to guide maps and fundraising materials. "One of our ideas was to create a dynamic symbol that isn't contained within a shape to reflect the growth and dynamism of the organization," explains principal Ken Carbone.

FIRST, DO NO HARM

Too often, designers fall into the trap of trying to do too much. Even when change is called for, as in five examples mentioned previously (and seen in great detail elsewhere in this

Light Touch. Carbone Smolan's solution for Brooklyn Botanic Garden demonstrates a skilled, light hand. It transformed an overgrown, congested identity into a clear and well-kept garden while still maintaining the most fundamental element of the original design: the botanic idyllic.

book), wholesale change would be folly. It takes wisdom, experience, and restraint to create evolutionary change. And real change is not necessarily in a new logo but how that logo lives and grows within its native environment over time.

Brian Collins put it this way: "My concern is we still are obsessed with the craft of making a logo, without realizing that the real craft—and the real work, and the real intelligence—is in giving that identity life, so it moves across communications and environments and products. That is the work. The real craft is the system, not the object."

Restraint. Patience. Work. So the next time Delta or KFC or Toyota gives you a shout to redefine their moribund brands, try to curb your enthusiasm, right? Try not to think of the millions you will be billing and the hundreds you will have to hire. Try, instead, to put their interests first. Follow the Hippocratic corpus, as though were you a physician, not just a smart graphic designer: First, do no harm.

Debbie Millman

Sterling Platinum

DESIGN: STERLING BRANDS
NEW YORK

Q: I wanted to talk to you about redesigning logos. Let's say a client comes to you and says, "I want you to take a look at my logo—I think it is getting a little tired." How do you begin the logo refreshment or replacement process?
DM: Here, we first ask this question: "Why change it now?" It is critical that you understand their motivation for change and the organization's vision to guide your approach. This helps understand what their definition of "change" really is. Revolutionary change? Evolutionary change?

I have had a senior officer tell me they wanted a revolutionary "game changer," a "new stake in the ground." We then delivered ideas that could do that and this person came back and said, "Oh, what we really meant by revolutionary change was going from light blue to dark blue." That's not revolutionary change to a designer, but it may be revolutionary to the client. Discover their motivation and vision first and then begin the redesign process.

Q: What happens when the reverse occurs, when the client asks for a revolution but, after your research, you return to and tell them, "Hey, what you've got is actually great. It has valuable equity. We recommend only minor change to the logo"?

Nice Buns. Don't touch those buns, research informed Debbie Millman, who told us a designer could have put just about any words between BK's golden buns and consumers would still read it as "Burger King." But without some contemporary elements, it might also come to be read as stale bread and dead meat.

DM: It's never the same for any given project. The same circumstances never occur. Even brands within the same category don't have the same issues. So, if we're being asked to create a new identity, you must first understand what is working with that identity. It's not about change for change sake, it's about what can we do to make this identity better and create a better understanding of it? We often conduct external research to determine which brand characteristics are strong and which are weak. Once we do this, we can then know where improvements can be made, including visual, philosophical, and messaging. The mark is the visual representation of the brand, signaling values and affiliations. Our job is to communicate those values and affiliations as best as possible. But the designer must understand what those values and affiliations are before she starts trying to communicate them. That is upfront work and it is necessary.

BURGER KING

DRIVE THRU

BURGER KING

Q: So, do the due diligence first, right? Then do you have a one-size-fits-all process or do you tailor it for every client?

DM: Yes, and yes. Sterling Brands has a process and equity evaluation tool that we use. But we tailor our process to fit each case. We always begin the journey on a familiar path, but what happens along the way is always different. The road map starts with understanding what the brand's diagnostics and current marketplace situation are. We then plot a course for where the brand or identity can go in the future. We develop stimuli to test with consumers to assess their point of view. Remember, with any brand goals or brand value statements, there are a number of ways to visualize and bring them to life. In tests, we gauge consumer reaction, but not for specifics on things like color or the way it needs to be portrayed on the package, but more their emotional reactions. This helps remove some of the subjectivity when evaluating design. Design is not empirical; it's subjective, so you must begin with a sound strategy: understand the current marketplace and consumer point of view in order to remove as much of the subjectivity as possible.

Q: That's a big toolkit—and the removal of as much subjectivity as possible in design evaluation seems to be major component of it. Okay, so let's talk about another whopper—or, rather, Burger King, a whopper of a brand. Tell us about that experience …

were they a new client when you began evaluating their brand?

DM: Yes. They wanted a new visual strategy that signaled the changes they were making to the brand vision and brand experience.

Q: Were they looking to expand into other food categories?

DM: They wanted a visual identity aligned with their organization values and the kind of food customers experienced when they walked into their stores. They wanted an identity that was more engaged, energetic, and modern. Their existing logo hadn't been redesigned in more than thirty years. It was two bun halves with the words "Burger King" in between. It was a tad dusty and needed refreshing.

Nice Assets. The mark created by Sterling Brands maintains valuable equity while thrusting Burger King forward. The type remains thick and juicy, the palette is less mustard-and-ketchup—and most importantly, the mark's tilt lends energy and dimension. People don't "read" logos, contends Millman, "they assess them." (Before: opposite page, left, After: opposite page, center)

Q: Was this existing logo the original logo?

DM: No. There was a slight change in the logo that was created. The previous redesign just made the two halves of the bun the same size (previously, the top half was larger). It is astonishing so much effort went into changing the bun size. At the time our creative director commented, "What are you guys, a bread company?" His point was to celebrate the fact that they were and are fast-food company, and with a flagship sandwich: the Whopper. We wanted to celebrate those facts. We did some eye-tracking tests with consumers. We discovered that we could put "Mick Hodgson" between the buns and, by testing in one- or two-second increments, consumers still thought they were seeing "Burger King" because the identity was so iconic. Here's a poorly kept secret: people don't actually read logos, they assess them. What this eye-tracking research told us was that we had to keep the integrity of the mark intact—we needed evolution, not revolution. People still wanted those buns.

Q: I like the idea of "Mick Hodgson" between buns, really, whole wheat or white. So, describe your solution …

DM: We activated the logo. We gave it energy by adding the blue palette to the disc device orbiting the buns. We eliminated the "me, too" color palette of many prominent fast-food companies—red and yellow or red and gold—but kept some of the "bubbly" shape of the type that was iconic to the brand. Some of it. Because we then sharpened typographic edges, then tilted it, giving it much more energy and dimension. We didn't get rid of those buns, either.

Q: OK, enough about burgers. Let's talk health food market. That has changed dramatically in the past years with high consumer consciousness on locally grown, healthier, organic foods. Describe the brief Celestial Seasonings presented to your team.

DM: Simple: they wanted to reintroduce their brand to a new generation of consumers. They created the herbal tea category and owned it for a long time. The brand itself began in a serendipitous manner. The founder,

who lived in Boulder, Colorado, picked some berries and herbs and made tea from them. From there, it all just took off, first with Sleepytime and then, before they knew it, a hundred different skews. Later, Kraft bought it. Then Hain bought it from Kraft and renamed it Hain Celestial. It had become out of date and difficult to find on the shelf with so many flavors and tea types—black tea, white tea, red tea, green tea, caffeinated, decaffeinated, zingers. They needed a segmentation system as well as a redesign.

Q: Makes me jittery just thinking about it. So, what did you come up with?

DM: First, we were told everything was on the table. Then, three-fourths of the way through the project, we were told we had to use the existing illustrations because money was not available to commission all new illustrations. Then we learned that the illustrations were actually original paintings being stored at corporate. Viewing them, we realized most had been cropped beyond recognition. We recommended they

Ommm. Sterling Brands discovered that the original Celestial illustrations were still in the company archives, but over the years most had been cropped beyond recognition. Those that didn't, appear dated—and that retained a spiritual, cosmic-y kind of feeling—were reintroduced in new packaging, opening up the opportunity to make dramatic changes to the logo. (Before: top, After: bottom)

open up the pack and feature these beautiful illustrations—but a specific type of illustration. Anything with people in it that appeared nostalgic didn't work. The illustrations had to have a spiritual, cosmicy kind of feeling.

Q: The new logo basically changes the name of the brand, doesn't it? Now it's Celestial.

DM: That was intentional. That's what people call the brand. *Celestial* is a beautiful word. It's a really magnificent word. Every company should be so lucky to have a word that is so special. The word *seasonings* takes you to a different place emotionally: salt and

pepper, and saffron, and paprika—not what the company is about. But tests showed taking the word *seasonings* away entirely went too far. And it was important that there be some recognition of the heritage of the brand and

the name. So we minimized *seasonings* and took the opportunity to play with the word *celestial*.

Q: You mentioned segmentation—you created subcategories, right?

DM: No. We created a messaging system that made it easier for consumers to find what they wanted using color and typography.

Q: Debbie, you have worked on some well-loved brands. When you touch brands people love, there is much risk. And responsibility.

DM: You are correct. We tend to do work on heritage brands, that's one of our specialties—when something's been in the market for a long time, whether people like it or don't like it is almost irrelevant to anybody but designers. People are comfortable with it because this is the way it's expected to look. There needs to be an understanding of heritage and history that transcends whether or not someone's comfortable with the kerning.

A perfect example of this is Tropicana. People rely on Tropicana in their daily lives. But when something you rely on day to day changes in the middle of the biggest financial collapse since the Great Depression, perhaps no matter how good the package or bad the package is, people are resistant. The quality of design is irrelevant. The fact was the rest of the world was collapsing around them. I think that in many ways they projected their feelings about change and insecurity and vulnerability onto something as silly as what they were drinking in the morning because that was the only thing they could rebel against and feel like their voices could be heard.

Q: Are there any logo redesigns that you love?

DM: Duffy's Bahamas identity is one of my favorites.

Q: How often have you been asked to redesign a logo that had been designed by someone you had a lot of respect for?

DM: Oh, we had to redesign the Kleenex logo, which was really hard. I believe it was done by Saul Bass. And I also was nervous when we redesigned the Hershey bar because it had never been redesigned in the sixty-five years of its existence.

Q: So was there ever a point on that one then that you said, "It's 65 years old—you shouldn't touch it, everyone loves it"?

DM: They were going to change it anyway because they were really concerned about tamper evidence after 9/11, so the existing pack with the little maroon sleeve that you pulled off had to be changed. I felt huge responsibility in making sure that the integrity of that pack was maintained. And I

Island Style. Millman loves Duffiy's redesign for the Islands of the Bahamas.

know that Michael Beirut hates it and was sobbing when he saw it.

Q: Well now, change is difficult. Maybe some of Michael's redesigns have broken other people's hearts.

DM: I take comfort in your words.

BURGER KING
DESIGN DIRECTOR: JAMES GRANT
CREATIVE DIRECTOR: MARCUS HEWITT

CELESTIAL SEASONINGS
DESIGN DIRECTOR: GERARD RIZZO
CREATIVE DIRECTOR: SIMON LINCE
ART DIRECTOR: CARLA VELASCO PALMER
PRODUCT ARTIST: SUSAN GIRLING

THE ISLANDS OF THE BAHAMAS
DESIGN: DUFFY & PARTNERS

CHAPTER 3: SLIGHT OF HAND (EVOLUTION)

CHAPTER 4

Revolutions

SOMETIMES THE, ONLY THING A BRAND NEEDS IS A LITTLE REFRESHING. But sometimes that's not enough. You simply have to start over. Many small and large branding examples that were submitted for this book were revolutions, not evolutions of the brand. They were fundamentally different from the previous identity. They were beyond the extent of our thesis. Then we reconsidered.

Even drastic change in an identity still requires the assessment and assignment of equity, even if that assignment is to the rubbish bin of history. But no matter how far you try distance yourself from the past, it's still there. A drastically altered identity is the mirror opposite of its predecessor. For every thesis there is antithesis.

Moreover, there is more to identity than the visual elements: things such as reputation, legacy, care, and quality shape perception as much as ugly, dated logos do. The experience consumers have with a product or service always trumps the identity design. People are forgiving if the logo color isn't to their liking, but they likely won't return or repurchase a product if they had a bad experience. But when massive change is called for, the single best way to signal change is to communicate with an entirely new logo and identity system. What follows are some interesting examples of precisely this.

There are common reasons why an old logo, logotype, or identity system is too tired to keep. Mergers and acquisitions rarely result in a blurring of identities as you see in Epic/Lincolnshire out of England—one's got to go. Delta's identity will eventually eclipse that of Northwest Airlines, a beloved brand in Minneapolis.

Typically, with mergers and acquisitions, one identity subsumes the other: Wells Fargo's new identity system will gradually replace Wachovia's. A true disaster can eliminate an identity: Air Florida became AirTrans after a tragic crash. Then again, some reasons are simply unpredictable, bizarre even.

Would you neglect your wardrobe for twenty years? Probably not. But that does not mean you need to start over. Well-timed evolutions of a logo or identity system can largely negate the need for drastic revolution down the road.

Timely changes can help you attract new ones and allow you to control perception rather than allowing perception to control you.

It's All Downhill. Would you neglect your wardrobe for twenty years? Timely updates to an identity can help bridge the generational differences between longtime users and New Age customers, whether they're alpine skiers or snowboarders. (Before: top left, After: bottom left)

CREATIVE DIRECTOR/DESIGNER/ILLUSTRATOR:
BRYAN MCCLOSKEY

ICEFALL
LODGE

ADVENTURE FOR ALL SEASONS

GOLDEN, B.C. • WWW.ICEFALL.CA

Connie Birdsall
and Brendán Murphy

You Get What You Need

Q: I'd like to talk to you about some of the projects you've worked on, and in doing so, talk to you about your general approach about what happens when a client comes to you and says, "We want to redesign our logo." What process do you use to evaluate whether that is appropriate or not?

CB: A huge part of our business is just figuring out what the right identity relationships should be. Almost all of the clients that we've worked with face complex issues: they've either acquired other products and services, or developed them internally, but the presentation of those relationships visually can be challenging to communicate. Often, our role is to streamline this process and figure out systems and levels of communications that help get a company organized. Then we give them the tools they will need the next time similar circumstances arise.

As far as process goes, it is quite simple but thorough. The first step is to understand where they've come from, where they are, and where they are going. This involves taking a look at the competitive marketplace, understanding what their audiences know about them, and understanding what they should know about that company. We seek the gaps between perceptions versus reality.

Q: So the goal is to close the gaps, not mind them?

CB: The goal is to figure out what it is that they want to change or need to change in order to communicate more clearly about who they are and where they're going. Companies come to us for different reasons. Sometimes they're being spun off, such as the case with Ameriprise, which was spun off from American Express Financial Services. Here is a Fortune 500 company that one day woke up and found that they were going to communicate to their customers and prospects without the American Express name. The solution had to be ready in six months.

Q: Six months? That was fast, wasn't it?

BM: Originally the schedule was six months—then it got condensed into three months. And the focus was a name that would not alienate their valuable advisor network.

CB: Their advisor network is critical to them. The new name had to carry with it some of the equity of American Express. Ameriprise emerged and it was based upon "the compass for your financial future." This is where the symbol came from.

BM: Another reason companies come to us is mergers. When two huge companies come together, it can be political and complex because most of the time there's great equity in both of the identities. It's incredibly rare when two companies come together that they throw out everything and start from scratch with a completely new name and logo. So that's always a particularly interesting project, but one that we really do study carefully—the equities from both companies must be accounted for and usually built into the new brand identity. It is rare that you throw out everything and start from scratch.

No Fault Divorce. What happens when you wake up one day and discover your business no longer carries the name of one of the biggest financial service players in the world? You find a way—fast—to assure your most valuable advocates that the more things change, the more the stay the same. Lippincott helped Ameriprise do that.
(Before: top, After: bottom)

Q: Why is that rare nowadays?

CB: Because building recognition and identity in the marketplace is tremendously costly. Great brand equity is too valuable to set out at the curb on merge day.

Q: What other reasons do big birds come to roost at Lippincott? You certainly get your fair share of the biggest …

CB: Perception gaps: something has changed dramatically at their business but they are perceived for something else—something that they no longer do. Or they do it, but they want to reach into new markets and those markets do not realize this company can meet their needs, too. They need to be repositioned. Meredith is a perfect example of that: they were moving from a traditional magazine publishing business model to a much broader media platform. They had to send that message out.

Q: Let's briefly discuss two: Intuit and Wells Fargo. Tell us about the changes Lippincott made to these famous brands. What did they need and how did you solve their problem with these solutions?

BM: Our work for Wells Fargo started before the Wachovia merger. We didn't work on their logo—the logo is the red box—we worked on the stagecoach, which is their corporate signature. In the past they had been, as they called it, "promiscuous" with their famous stagecoach. It was inconsistently used across their print collateral and online applications. They had photographic stagecoaches, silhouettes of stagecoaches,, and they had commissioned numerous illustrated versions, including those of Michael Schwab and Mark Summers.

Q: Did Mark Summers do that woodcut version?

BM: Yes, he created the wood engraving version for Wells Fargo. Schwab's illustration was never used as part of the identity; it was used as an anniversary poster series. Much of that work was excellent. As part of the rebranding process, the question was asked, "We have this beautiful heritage element but what does it mean for today?" So [for] young adults, what did the stagecoach mean? We wanted the stagecoach to have meaning for newer and younger audiences, of course. The kernel of our idea was that the stagecoach has been "here for you now and over time." It stays with us. It's tied to the quality of service.

When we looked at redesigning the stagecoach we went into research to figure out what people saw in the stagecoach. We created different renderings, both photographic and illustrative. We showed side views, three quarter views, and front views. Each had differ-

Together we'll go far

ent meaning to people. There was a big question of whether the stagecoach should go from right to the left, or left to right. When we showed the older versions, people thought it appeared as if it wasn't going to stop for them or it was running away from them versus coming towards them. So the research really helped to identify the orientation of the stagecoach and the meaning of it. We did a full on series of rendering styles around the stagecoach— everything from the traditional painterly approach; everything from Japanese animated styles to Felix Stockwell's line art styles. I guess the best way to describe the process was an absolute and complete study of possibilities and equities of the stagecoach.

Child's Play. The Wells Fargo stagecoach is not a logo. It is, according to Lippincott, a heritage device that stays with us. So how do you make such a device resonate with newer and younger audiences? Hire an old-school guy (John Rush) who's accomplished "quite a bit of work with children's books rendering horses." Bring a whip, too. (Before: opposite page, After: above)

Q: Who wound up doing the final rendering we see today?
BM: John Rush, who works in Chicago and teaches now and again at the Art Academy in San Francisco. He was teaching in San Francisco at the time, so we sent him to meet and talk to the folks at Wells Fargo. They liked his style, they liked the heroic quality of his work, and research had shown that consumers liked his style. I think it was helpful that he had done quite a bit of work with children's books rendering horses. He's like an old commercial artist type of guy.

Q: Let's shift gears to Intuit. What equity from the previous mark did you keep?
BM: Intuit was a bit of a different story. It was a brand that was under-utilized. I guess the best analogy is a holding company kind of model. Intuit operated like a P&G where it had a stable of well-known, successful brands like QuickBooks and Quicken and TurboTax. People knew the brands, but didn't know about Intuit. The onset of the free online had radically changed Intuit's business model. They saw their opportunity in developing an entirely new brand for small business, where most of the business in the U.S. now resides.

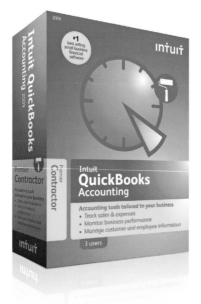

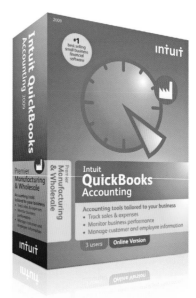

We helped them understand that what was needed was not a new brand, but a better leverage with the existing Intuit brand. First, the existing identity, dot matrix head and logotype, was dated and time stamped. It didn't necessarily talk to empowering small businesses. Some felt it meant old technology like dot matrix printers. The color itself was burgundy some associate with traditional, stodgy old banking, expensive, and foreign to Intuit's culture and perspective.

Q: We use QuickBooks all the time, but I would have never known it was an Intuit brand. Was creating that association a primary consideration?

BM: Yes, a big consideration. At first, their big brands like QuickBooks and TurboTax were off limits. But through research, everyone realized that the people using these products at home were using them for business purposes, too. It was a great opportunity to link between the corporate brand Intuit and the individual product brands.

I think the other thing that's happened is that they've built their portfolio around a broader offering than purely tax and accounting software. They're building up a portfolio of brands and services that are centered on small businesses. QuickBooks itself had people view it in a narrow way and it didn't have the legs to expand it into other services, so that's where the need to develop this other brand came from.

Q: So on this packaging you've got three QuickBooks packages and then you've got Intuit QuickBooks and Intuit Payroll; is that an attempt for people to use the brand name in conjunction with the product name in the same way that people refer to Photoshop as Adobe Photoshop?

BM: As part of any project like this we often develop a migration path. It's important that we don't let go of any existing equities. So for example, with QuickBooks, one of their brand cues is the color green. So right out of the gate, even though Intuit was going to be a blue brand, we knew that people associated QuickBooks with green and that we should continue to leverage that in the short term but over time they wanted to see how QuickBooks could migrate into a more Intuit visual system, if you like. So we developed a migration path with how they would get there.

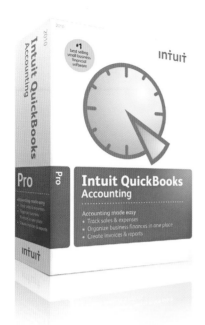

Q: I have one last question for you and Brendan. Do you ever wish you could design a logo for your local bike or coffee shop? Just once?

CB: We try to encourage our people to get involved with smaller, interesting projects.

BM: If you read the designer blogs, Lippincott typically gets bashed because we haven't delivered the best thing since sliced bread, but people don't understand the various challenges that go into building an identity. The fun of it is a complexity. We all do logos for our brothers and sisters and such, but when you get into these big undertakings, basically all your senses are challenged, all your education is challenged, you work more in a team setting, and that's what makes it fun. You can't always get what you want.

White or Wheat? "If you read the designer blogs, Lippincott typically gets bashed because we haven't delivered the best thing since sliced bread," says Brendán Murphy. "We all do logos for our brothers and our sisters but when you get into these big undertakings, basically your senses [and education] are challenged."
(Before: above, After: below)

AMERIPRISE
CREATIVE DIRECTOR: CONNIE BIRDSALL, BRENDÁN MURPHY
DESIGNERS: BRENDÁN MURPHY, JENNIFER LEHKER
COPYWRITING: BRENDÁN MURPHY
PRODUCTION: BRENDAN DEVALLANCE, JEREMY DARTY

MEREDITH
CREATIVE DIRECTOR: CONNIE BIRDSALL
ART DIRECTOR: JENIFER LEHKER
DESIGNERS: JENNIFER LEHKER, SANDRA HILL, BRENDÁN MURPHY
PRODUCTION: BRENDAN DEVALLANCE, JEREMY DARTY

INTUIT
CREATIVE DIRECTOR, DESIGNER: BRENDÁN MURPHY
PRODUCTION: BRENDAN DEVALLANCE, JEREMY DARTY
STRATEGY: MICHAEL D'ESOPO, KATHERINE GLASS, SARAH BELLAMY

WELLS FARGO
CREATIVE DIRECTORS: BRENDÁN MURPHY (LIPPINCOTT), BRIAN STILL (WELLS FARGO)
DESIGNERS: BRENDÁN MURPHY, CHRISTIAN DIERIG
ILLUSTRATOR: JOHN RUSH
PRODUCTION: BRENDAN DEVALLANCE, JEREMY DARTY

UPS LOGO: CROSSING THE GREAT DIVIDE

RECYCLING & REDSIGNING LOGOS

IT'S A FINE LINE BETWEEN LOVE AND HATE

"The original UPS shield implied meaning with special attention to care with that tied ribbon. Sure, one might argue that it is not related to modern, logistical delivery and all that modern stuff, but it just seemed to me to be timeless." **MICHAEL GERICKE**

"I'm a sucker for the clean and simple marks of the mid-twentieth century. I'm not so keen on anything that has been altered to be three-dimensional or shiny, just for the sake of doing it." **SEAN ADAMS**

"We have a great fondness for the old UPS logo." **3RD EDGE COMMUNICATIONS, NEW JERSEY**

"I really enjoy the redesign of UPS and Pringles." **BRAINBOX, PARANA BRAZIL**

"I would like to see Paul Rand's UPS mark brought back into use. The brown truck just isn't the same without it." **KEN CARBONE**

"I love the new UPS logo." **CAROL GARCIA DEL BUSTO, BARCELONA**

"The original UPS logo by Paul Rand captured the soul of UPS. The new logo lacks that and almost looks generic."
MARY HUTCHINSON, DESIGN SEATTLE

"Definitely bring back the original UPS logo. The gradations and Logo 2.0 look has little personality or conceptual meaning."
NANCY WU, VANCOUVER, BC

"UPS and Northwest Airlines are a couple that should never have been touched. I don't like either of them at all."
JOEL TEMPLIN, SAN FRANCISCO

"I'm very fond of the old UPS symbol." **CONNIE BIRDSALL**

"Bring back the old UPS logo. Although years after he did it, Paul Rand was not satisfied with the lettering and approached UPS with a recommended update. They declined." **ALEX ISLEY**

"I would like to see the Mobil Oil Pegasus, UPS, and the AT&T logos brought back into use." **BILL GRANT**

"I like the UPS redesign. It must have been difficult to update a Paul Rand classic, but the new one works—
it recalls the original and repositions the company in a contemporary manner." **MICHAEL CARABETTA**

"I still like the old UPS logo. I'm a big fan of the old Mobil gas logo with Pegasus." **TERRY MARKS**

"I remember Emily Oberman of Number 17 saying how disappointed she was when the UPS logo was redesigned.
She asked their UPS driver for his shirt with the old logo on it." **MICHAEL HODGSON**

"I never liked the Rand logo. It reminded me of Christmas. And we never had Christmas when I was a child." **MATT PORTER**

Keep On Truckin'. Before: opposite, After: above

SECTION 2: Case Studies

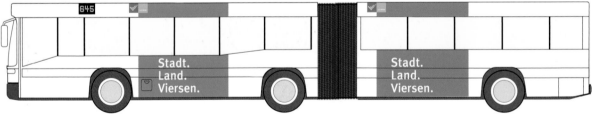

Stadt Viersen, Germany
Ausgezeichnet!

MIRCO KURTH AT 28 LIMITED BRAND IN BOCHUM, GERMANY, approaches rebranding "cautiously," he says. Caution must have served Kurth especially well when his firm redesigned the identity for Viersen, Germany, a town of about 75,000 in the state of North Rhine-Westphalia. (The city of Viersen is the capital of the district that also bears its name.)

Kurth, who founded 28 Limited Brand in 2004, was asked to help develop a new logo and logotype for the city of Viersen. The existing logo was actually a coat of arms featuring three emblems which, according to legend, represented the three formerly independent towns that now comprise modern Viersen: Süchteln, Dülken, and Viersen.

Says Mirco Kurth, "The biggest challenge for us was in creating a symbol that could represent an entire city. You can imagine, many eyes were watching us, especially Viersen's own citizens."

This design would have to speak for them all.

CAREFUL NOW

Besides being under the critical watch of an entire town, there was for Kurth another challenge, more mundane but just as difficult: "The letterhead. Every designer wants to make the letterhead beautiful, but town officials just want it to be functional. Creating a letterhead that met their satisfaction and met our design standards was particularly difficult in comparison with other design applications."

Ah, bureaucrats. Most couldn't care less how the city's identity appeared on cultural infrastructure, office buildings, information kiosks, city vehicles, official uniforms, tourist promotional materials, or even Google Maps. But

Kein Sissy. In replacing a musty coat of arms with an abstract identity intended to convey new meaning about a district and its capital city, 28 leading Limited Brand invited the wrath of conservative citizens and the village tax collector. Who says graphic design is for the faint of heart? (Before: above, After: right)

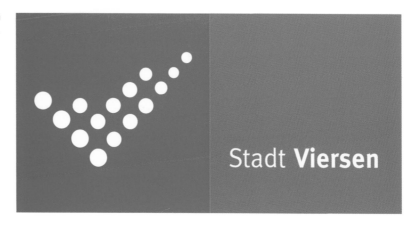

they wanted to be sure that every citizen of Viersen got a good-looking tax bill. God love them.

Kurth built consensus by keeping the client informed at every step and by conducting a workshop that made clear what the new identity could accomplish—and what it could not.

STRIKING A BALANCE

Naturally, the city of Viersen had a sound business reason behind the decision to catapult the coat of arms outside the city walls: to attract commerce. To do this, Viersen's identity needed to celebrate its open spirit and its distinctive traditions, including the Eier & Speck (Egg and Bacon) Indie Rock/Alternative/Punk Music Festival and its annual jazz festival. Moreover,

the identity needed to suggest a place where things come together, where people connect through commercial and recreational interests to do mighty things.

A tattered old coat of arms screamed Renaissance, not *renaissance*—it had to go. The solution created by Kurth is a giant leap forward. Everything about the town's identity changed.

In some instances, the new identity includes these three words beneath: "Stadt. Land. Viersen." Translated literally this means "City. Country. Viersen." The slogan, used in some but not all applications, sums up the new identity: Viersen—Stadt and Land, city and country, town and surrounding district—offers both urban and bucolic pleasures, making it a great place to connect with other people.

"The new identity consists of two squares side by side, one blue, the other green," Kurth explains. "Blue stands for the urban, vibrant character of the city of Viersen. Green represents the peaceful character of greater Viersen, the district—especially its healthfulness, vitality, abundance of nature and recreation. Two points join (networking, connection) to form a stylized *V*, which can be seen as an upward hook."

CHECKLIST

Kurth's identity is a minor triumph because he trumped the provincial small-mindedness that sinks some places into eternal obscurity. "It is difficult for a small city to do something new. And we know not everyone will understand every nuance of the new symbol and layout," Kurth admits. "It would take a lot of money to educate them on its context, meaning, and purpose." But many here do believe that the new logo sets Viersen apart from other regional cities by suggesting its advantages such as natural beauty and urban networking opportunities. "This will set it apart and if it does, we have done everything right," he notes.

Ganz toll! (Well done!)

DESIGN DIRECTOR, COPYWRITER: MIRCO KURTH

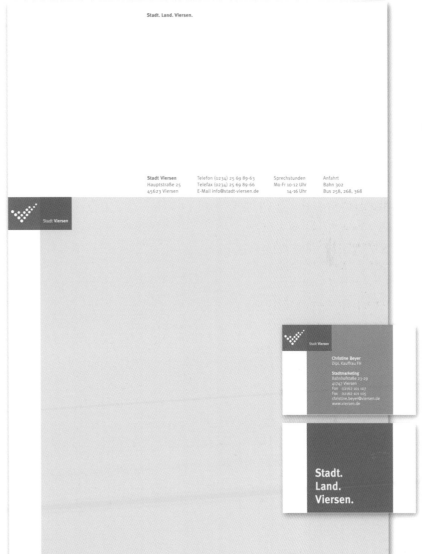

Broad Minded. The Stadt Viersen identity is a minor triumph because it trumps provincial small-mindedness and puts the city in position to trumpet attributes that will attract population and business. Says designer Mirco Kurth, "This will set them apart."

Play It Again. This worldwide fashion brand's signature identity element is not the famous Paul Smith signature. It is instead the company's strategically deployed stripe pattern, first used in 1997 by designer Alan Aboud. Of the stripe, Aboud says, "It just struck a chord with me. It seemed very simple, very bright, very colorful, but very elegant at the same time."

CASE STUDY
Paul Smith
Striped Teas and Other Goodies

DESIGN: ABOUD CREATIVE
LONDON

THE FAMILIAR PAUL SMITH SIGNATURE LOGO IS NOT, IN FACT, PAUL SMITH'S SIGNATURE. It was drawn by Zena Marsh, a friend in the early '70s for Smith's first hometown shop, a hundred-square-foot (9.3 m^2) space on Nottingham's Byard Lane. Now, Paul Smith shops literally span the globe, with hundreds of shops worldwide.

The signature logo "was never intended to be anything other than a mark," says Alan Aboud, principal, creative director Aboud Creative.. "It's a tremendously tricky device to use. It works small and discreet, or massive; any kind of middle ground just looks a bit awkward. It's only with experience that you know how big it should be or how small it should be."

The hand-drawn logo was tightened up a little in the early 1980s when Smith opened his first shop in London, on Floral Street; the third and current incarnation of the logo stands from 1989, the year Aboud fresh from St. Martin's School of Art, first worked for Smith.

After a few years of using second- or third-generation bromide versions, Aboud had the logo redrawn so it could be used on a Mac, taking that occasion to "smooth out the roughness, lend clarity, and beef it up." For all intents and purposes, few could notice the modifications other than a true Paul Smith follower.

MORE STRIPES THAN A ZEBRA

The Paul Smith 1997 men's collection included a shirt in a colorful multi-stripe. Although they didn't realize it at the time, the pattern became bigger than anything they could imagine.

By then the company was known for color, print, and passion, and was especially credited with restoring color to men's wardrobes—but at the same time it had a public persona that was basically monochromatic. Aboud Creative was asked to reinvent the corporate packaging.

(Before: right, above; After: right, below)
The only record that shows the old logo is a photograph (taken by a customer) of this boy in Kenya who kept all his possessions in this bag.

When Aboud came across the multi-stripe print in his research, he says, it "just struck a chord," and he used it as a selling card for that season's collection. "It just seemed very simple, very bright, very colorful, but very elegant at the same time."

This feeling led to the production of a range of carrier bags using the same stripe. Envisioned as a limited-edition run, the vibrant bags "kind of took off, in an unprecedented way," as Aboud puts it. The multistripe was a smash—"so much so, that we were actually quite scared by the success of it," Aboud says. "Everyone wanted to use

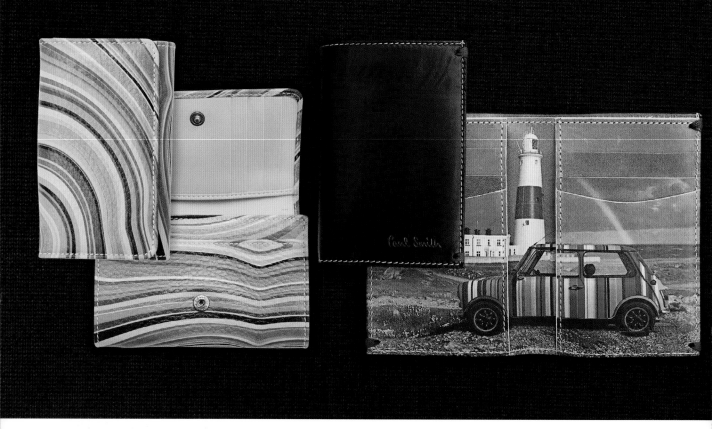

it, whether it be for socks, cuff links, whatever. We really studiously controlled the usage of the stripe until we came to the conclusion that there was longevity in the stripe and people really wanted it. And it went on from there."

Indeed, it went on. In 1999, the company introduced a variation for women: the swirl stripe, a simple twist of the design by Aboud's senior designer, Maxine Law. This took off even more, becoming one of the biggest sellers in the women's collection for accessories. Wallets, handbags, and leather goods still carry the swirl print today, and they still sell in bucket loads.

THE SINCEREST FORM OF FLATTERY. "When people see the stripes, they automatically think of PS," Aboud notes. It's an association that imitators have rushed to exploit. For Aboud and Paul Smith, that means stripes gone wild. "It's insane, the amount of material that has come out since the multistripe arrived," says Aboud, who dryly admits: "Initially, it was a pain in the ass." The company has sent cease-and-desist orders to many of the more blatant borrowers of the multistripe, including John Lewis, Crate and Barrel in the U.S., and Paper Chase.

Aboud muses, "It was never intended to be this kind of global phenomenon that it turned out to be. But I'm happy that I've done this, and I'm really happy that it's lasted this long and still looks fresh. As a designer that is the ultimate thing you want to do: to have something in your portfolio that *still looks good*."

Grotesque: the New Lovely. In some applications, the brand name appears in Grotesque Bold rather than Paul Smith script. "We've been lucky to have [it]," says Aboud of the grotesque version. "It takes the pressure off trying to brand things with the Paul Smith signature all the time."

Paul Smith

PAUL
SMITH

WWW.PAULSMITH.CO.UK

Please, Make It Stop. The stripe motif is now a Paul Smith signature, but it did not start out that way. It was designed as a selling card for one season's collection. It led to production of a line of carrier bags with the stripe. Then, according to Aboud, it "kind of took off, in an unprecedented way; so much so, that we were actually quite scared by the success of it."

THE FINAL PART OF THE KIT

Around 1989, Aboud and Mario Testino shot the Paul Smith advertising campaigns, which featured the first use of Grotesque Bold for the company name in place of the famous signature. "The use of a sans serif has dipped in and out of use since then, but it's only in the past three years that we've really aggressively used it in all of our advertising," Aboud explains. The plain, heavy letters now appear on the packaging for Rose perfume and the just-launched Paul Smith Man.

"We've been lucky to have that type," Aboud says. "It's as powerful as the multi-stripe and it takes the pressure off trying to brand things with the Paul Smith signature all the time. The block type—the power of that type—is what people are recognizing as PS."

CLOSING THE CIRCLE

And now as the circle closes, it closes backwards—something that Smith would have a good laugh about, saying "Yeah! It's completely mad!"

On the label for Paul X, a jeans line for women, the logo *is* Paul Smith's handwriting—which has come to look exactly like the original signature logo because he's copied it a trillion times when signing things for 30 years plus. The same thing happened on a limited-edition Evian bottle that they have just designed. The man's signature is getting "ominously close" to his company's signature, jokes Aboud. "Out of repetition he's kind of morphing into himself, into the brand."

PAUL SMITH
DESIGN DIRECTOR/CREATIVE DIRECTOR:
ALAN ABOUD
DESIGNERS: LISA COMERFORD, CARL WELLMAN, MAXINE LAW.

EVIAN
CREATIVE DIRECTION AND DESIGN: SIR PAUL SMITH
DESIGN DIRECTOR: ALAN ABOUD

Teatro Nacional Sucre

Bocca Tango
Julio Bocca

Cantantes,
Orquesta y
Ballet Argentino.

Fundación
Teatro
Nacional
Sucre

Nov. **18** | 20h30
Nov. **19** | 18h00

Primera de Palcos $80
Segunda de Palcos $60
Platea $40
Luneta $20

Socios Diners 10% de descuento

www.teatrosucre.com

CASE STUDY

Teatro Nacional Sucre
Sweet Dreams are Made of This

DESIGN: LATIN BRAND
QUITO, ECUADOR

SANDRO AND SILVIO GIORGI OF LATINBRAND HAVE A GOOD THING GOING IN QUITO, ECUADOR. Their approach to branding is always on the mark, as can be seen in their work on behalf of Teatro Nacional Sucre, a cultural institution in this South American nation. It is a casebook example of evolving a brand by building a fresh new identity off the foundation of existing equity: their iconic neoclassical home building.

To mark its 120th birthday, directors at Teatro Nacional Sucre decided it was time rethink its communication system. They were confronting a problem common to venerable arts institutions: they needed to connect with younger audiences.

"One thing we all know, an old image that won't connect with a young audience is calling for change. But first we had to define the potential strengths and weaknesses of the existing identity in order to revitalize it and make it competitive," says Sandro. According to him, the theater had never had a well-defined brand. It had a name. It had various constructs of the name with icons, usually one centered on its beautiful neoclassical building. But there was never a system; the brand meandered. Under new leadership, the directors saw the necessity to reorganize and truly brand the institution as a powerful force in the cultural life of Quito.

Sandro says his main challenge was the fact that few Ecuadorean cultural intuitions have the money to invest in design or communication. "Cultural groups here invest little in a professional image; therefore, few have the experience working with design professionals, so we had to educate them."

This meant LatinBrand had to present their strategy and solution numerous times to various groups within the institution. "We had to explain to the managers why the changes were necessary and how they would apply to the new brand architecture and to their communications."

Neoclassics, Renewed. When the identity of an esteemed cultural instituion incorporates the most iconic architectural jewel in the city, it is prudent to find an identity system that puts those old stones to good purpose. Latinbrand of Quito, Ecuador, managed to do just that, building a fresh look on an ancient foundation. (Before: top, After: bottom)

TEATRO NACIONAL SUCRE

Despite numerous versions that did not include it, the directors would not let their neoclassic building go. It had to be part of the new image. Says Sandro, "The building was constructed in the late nineteenth century in the style of a Renaissance opera house. It is an architectural landmark here. At first, we tried to sell them on a mark that was strictly a logotype in a rectangle—easy to apply to the many different things they need such as coffee shops, retail, communication, etc. But the building was needed. This meant developing it into an icon that could be applied to many communication elements required in the future."

Strict simplicity was needed, not neoclassic flourishes. And it required one gigantic compromise: when the application is small or offers limited resolution, only the words *Teatro Nacional Sucre* are used in the rect-

angle. The logo is applied to many elements, including ticket office signage, invitations, and uniforms.

Whenever a designer is asked to change the look of a beloved—if bedraggled—cultural institution, there is much at stake. First, there are the new leaders wanting change. But around them are longtime fans, patrons, and employees resistant to

change. Then there is the public at large who—if not interested in the theater per se—feel they have a stake in the place due to its prominence as an architectural landmark in their city. What this new identity system accomplishes is not stunning, new design; rather, its glory is that the new identity moves a musty but vital cultural institution into the future. And that is tremendous.

Says Sandro, "We created a change to this logo with the hope that it will last another forty years. The essence of its brand—its past—has been honored. A cultural institution that honors its past will have a future."

DESIGN DIRECTOR: SANDRO GIORGI
CREATIVE DIRECTOR, ART DIRECTOR,
ILLUSTRATOR: SILVIO GIORGI

Not Your Grandma's Teatro. Initial versions of the design rendered the neoclassical building more Bauhaus than Renaissance. This was more than some at the Teatro officers could stomach. The final artwork, (above, bottom), restores the façade to *some* of its original glory but still maintains a contemporary look that says, "appropriate for younger audiences unaccompanied by ancestors."

"We created a change to this logo with the hope that it will last another forty years."

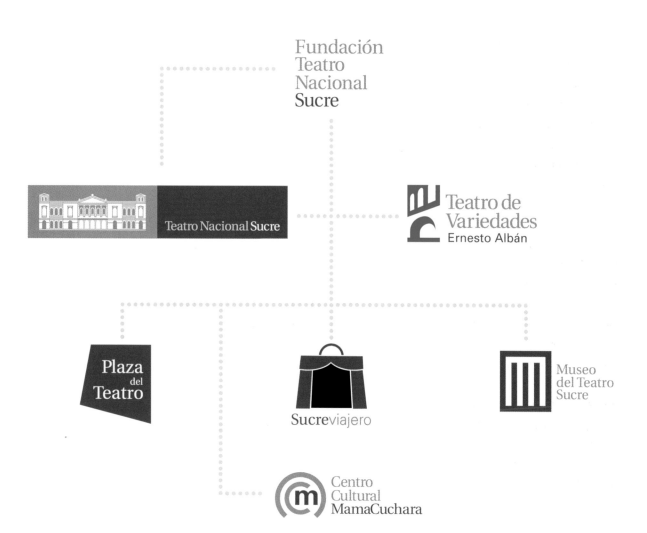

Distillerie di Franciacorta

The Lion, the Which, and the Wherefore

DESIGN: RANIERI DESIGN
BRESCIS, ITALY

AS THE VESPAS FLY BY NO. 3C VIA NAZARIO SAURO, near the intersection with Via Trento in the city of Brescia, Italy, some very memorable and effective design is going on inside Raineri Design. This firm submitted a number of breathtaking case studies, but it was their work for Distillerie Franciacorta that really caught our eye. It's a brilliant example of brand evolution. Distillerie Franciacorta was familiar with Raineri Design and so they approached William Raineri for a much-needed brand update and repositioning. The winemaker's logo, packaging, advertising, and identity system would all be redesigned.

"The logo and the rest of the identity no longer represented the brand," says Raineri. "The company was losing audience awareness and market share. It needed to reach a more diverse market."

Distillerie Franciacorta, located in Gussago, Italy, about 50 miles (80 km) west of Milan, has been in business for more than a century. The company makes a wide range of red and white wine, plus brandy, liqueurs, dessert, and sparkling wines.

The design group knew that the brand already had tradition and respectability. "This is a well-known brand," Raineri says. "one of the largest producers of wine in Italy. Also it's based in one of the most active wine-producing areas in Europe: Franciacorta."

The design team first looked at the history of the company and the many manifestations of the visual personality over

time. "The process began with historical research into the origins of the brand, including close looks at changes to the product line over the course of years," Raineri explains. "This allowed us to understand the core values of the company. Next, we studied the competitive marketplace to learn where our best opportunities for differentiation would lie."

Old Wine in a New Bottle. One of the largest producers of wine in one of the largest wine producing regions in Europe, Distillerie Franciacorta needed to respect its past but not soak in it. Raineri Design of Gussago, Italy came up with a solution that distills the brand to its essence with an identity that is restrained, sophisticated, and easier to reproduce on new products and packaging.
(Before: above, After: below)

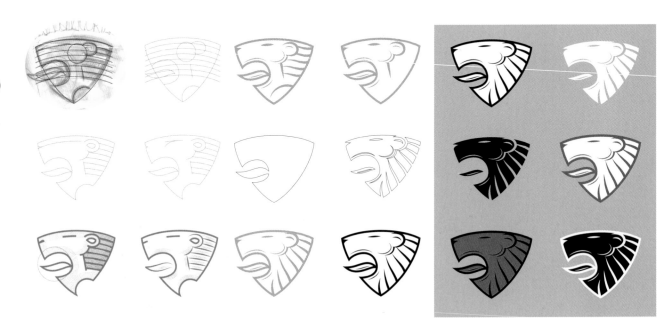

CLEANSING THE PALATE

After gaining all this knowledge, Raineri set it aside and, in his words, "concentrated on what Distillerie Franciacorta could become, not what it was! I wanted to cut all the baroque part of the brand to make it more modern and attractive."

Italians use a lot of exclamations when they talk. And Raineri had reason to be excited. This was going to lead to a beautiful solution for a revered brand. He determined the previous logo lacked three critical characteristics that the new design had to have: authority, memorability, and coherence with brand history.

THE VINTAGE

The redesign was dramatic. However, three key items were retained but redesigned: the lion and two complementary typefaces. "The lion belongs not only to Christian tradition, but in this region to political tradition, too," Raineri says. "After Venice conquered this region in the XV century, its symbol, the lion, became a symbol of power more than a symbol of faith." The word *distillerie* still appears as a hand-lettered font; the company name *Franciacorta* is still a more formal font.

"Our aim was to make the logo much more representative of Franciacorta's core values than its predecessor. We accomplish this by making the lion central to the logo, evolving it from a common full-body medieval lion into a more personalized lion—a head that is more graphic, more original, and much easier to reproduce in packaging. The historic references are there, but it is also more contemporary."

The final design is a reflection of that history—distilled, if you will, to the 'essence' of the Distillerie di Franciacorta. Is essence, as they say, the Holy

Grail of Design? Raineri has an answer: "Design is what you need to cover the 'last 10 golden centimeters,' those centimeters that separate the client from the pack."

"And *package*!" he adds. "The new design of Distillerie Franciacorta will be applied to *every* package. Simplicity is always a winning choice!"

And to that we say, *bellisimo*!!

DESIGN DIRECTOR, ART DIRECTOR, ILLUSTRATOR: WILLIAM RAINERI
PRODUCT ARTIST: MAURO CASSANI
COPYWRITER: GIANLUCA NAPPI

Holy Grail. Distilling a brand to its most essential—its essence—should be the Holy Grail of any designer. Says William Raineri, "Design is what you need to cover the last 10 golden centimeters— those which separate the client from the pack."

CASE STUDY

Chronicle Books

Showing Spine

DESIGN: CSK PARTNERS
SAN FRANCISCO

82

ONE DAY, MICHAEL CARABETTA WAS PASSING HIS BOSS ON THE STAIRCASE and his boss asked him, "Can we design a new logo?" Carabetta replied, "Sure." And so they did.

In the world of design, Chronicle Books is legend. Inspired by the "enduring magic" and importance of books, Chronicle's mission is, according to them, "to create books that are instantly recognizable for their creativity, spirit and value."

The current Chronicle spectacles logo has been appearing on the spine of its books since 1992, around the time it published its blockbuster bestseller, Nick Bantock's *Griffin & Sabine* (1991)—the book that really put Chronicle on the map with big-name publishers. The logo was created under the direction of then design director and current creative director Michael Carabetta. At that time, Chronicle was still part of the San Francisco Chronicle daily newspaper.

Foresight. Conceived and implemented in 1991, the logo for Chronicle Books has become, according to Carabetta, "a graphic shorthand for what we are," a goal attainable only through the consistent application of a very good logo over many, many years—a rare book indeed.

Carabetta says, "I had been thinking about the need to establish a graphic identity that better communicated the wit and savvy of our company and the joy of books in general. I had felt for some time that our old logotype did not graphically represent who we were (and are). It had no graphic presence, which is important on the spines of books."

When the client is you, you can please yourself—and fool yourself. You may assume that what you love others will, too. If your baby is objectively ugly, this is a disaster. But if your baby is objectively beautiful, everyone is delighted. Chronicle's spectacles logo is objectively delightful—and that's a beautiful thing.

But even an internal redesign needs some due diligence. Carabetta knew this. Working with CKS Partners, the design team conducted a series of interviews with the management team of Chronicle and initiated a visual audit of competitors. The research confirmed what Carabetta had already presumed: the vast majority of those surveyed agreed that the old logotype had become dated and inadequate. There was no equity left in it. It had to go.

"I had long felt that," Carabaretta says, "but our discovery exercise really confirmed it. We kept nothing from the previous design."

The old logotype was summarily swept into the rubbish bin of history; meanwhile the spectacles live on. The identity is now closing in on two decades of usefulness. And it looks as fresh, relevant, and joyful as a reminder of books as it was the day it debuted in the spring of 1992. The spectacles appear in marketing, sales promotions, and the web, but are seen primarily on the spines of millions of books on shelves around the world.

Chronicle Books is now 42—old enough to know better but still young enough to have fun. The company has expanded its online presence and selection of book gift packs, journals, how-to guides, and craft kits. It has a retail presence on trendy Union Street in San Francisco and in the lobby of its Second Street offices. In that store, one of the first things you will see after you walk through the door is a pair of familiar spectacles peeping amiably down at you, with no apparent owner but a readily apparent home.

The logo was devised to signal change at Chronicle Books many years ago. And it has survived, with distinctiveness and vigor intact, all the changes since. How? Carabetta explains the stamina of the specs:

"When we decided to change the logotype in 1991, Chronicle Books had grown from a small, regional-based publisher to one with international presence. That alone was reason enough to consider redesigning the brand identity. But even at that time our market reach had carried well beyond the bookstore—and this was prior to advent of the World Wide Web. The old logotype did not convey our sense of design, our quirky approach to book publishing, nor our entry into the non-book gift products arenas. And so it endures. And I think a key reason is that that the spectacles logo embodies our company credo that 'We See Things Differently,' that we have a vision. All things considered, it has worked for us across all media—in print and on the web. It has become a graphic shorthand for who we are."

Read that again: "It has become a graphic shorthand for who we are." Design doesn't get more farsighted than that.

DESIGN FIRM: CKS PARTNERS
DESIGN DIRECTOR: DANA SHIELDS
CREATIVE DIRECTOR: TOM SUITER
ART DIRECTOR: MICHAEL CARABETTA (FOR CLIENT)

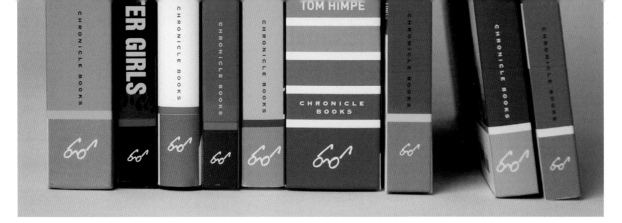

Before (right): Chronicle's former logotype had little personality and absolutely no mark.
After (far right): The addition of the reading glasses not only added a memorable device, it lent personality—the spectacles appear to belong to a contemplative mascot, who has left the room to get some tea.

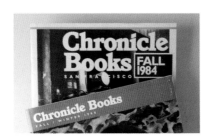

CASE STUDY
Mohawk Via
Paper Weight

DESIGN: ADAMSMORIOKA
BEVERLY HILLS

"SOMETIMES, IT'S A CHANGE IN CONTEXT THAT MAKES A REDESIGN NECESSARY," says Sean Adams, partner at AdamsMorioka. "Whether the logo changes or not, it's almost always the case that the context drives the work." AdamsMorioka's updated visual personality for Mohawk Via excels at one of the hardest tasks a designer can face: addressing a major change in context while enhancing an existing product's qualities.

Via grew rapidly following its acquisition by Mohawk Fine Papers. With an expanded product line and stronger marketing presence, Via was no longer the humble paper promotion it had been when AdamsMorioka designed its original logo; it was now a full-on business venture.

"You don't redesign an identity just to make something look better," Adams says. "You redesign to send the signal that the product or the owner or something significant has changed." This change met that standard.

HUB AND SPOKE

According to Adams, "The designer's role is to clarify the unifying message of their client's business." The new Mohawk Via mark emits admirable, elegant clarity: its hub-and-spoke configuration, with the line's selection of finishes and tones extending from a central brand, represents both the new importance and the new variety of the revamped Via line in a single image. "Because Via had become such a large line, we knew we had to help customers make distinctions between the finishes. Simplifying the mark and putting it at the center of the Via world was part of the solution," Adams says. "Adding the Mohawk name in the center was a conscious choice reflecting the overall business decision."

Before (left): AdamsMorioka designed the original identity for Via 101, a paper promotion that exhibited a tongue-in-cheek, slightly kitschy personality.
After (right): The redesigned Mohawk Via logo reflects a change in context for the Via name, as the paper line became a more important part of Mohawk Fine Papers' portfolio. The hub-and-spoke configuration has a consistent central element surrounded by secondary elements that visually evolve in various applications, but always portray the line's extensive array of finishes and tones.

The Mohawk Via operator's manual is among "the most comprehensive paper promotions out there," notes Sean Adams of AdamsMorioka. It provides a vast amount of information for designers working in the print medium. As in other Mohawk Via promotions, the operator's manual facilitates the emergence of a new visual personality for the line by varying secondary elements of the logo—the spokes—while the central hub remains consistent.

MOHAWK VELLUM
is now part of Via Vellum

**MOHAWK SATIN AND
VIA ULTRA SMOOTH**
are now part of Via Satin

MOHAWK TOMOHAWK
is now part of Via Felt

Via Vellum

via SATIN

VIA FELT

digital

digital

via

digital

VIA LINEN

VIA SMOOTH

Via Laid

Via 25% Cotton

THE VIA FAMILY
When Via joined Mohawk Fine Papers in 2005
it gained a powerful ally. Mohawk has been bringing
water and pulp together to make some of the highest
quality papers for decades. Dipping into Mohawk's
pool of knowledge has expanded Via's product line
and made it even better.

Freedom of Choice

Choice is the single major factor in creating successful printed pieces. Just like software, where the ability to navigate quickly and seamlessly is paramount, being able to choose among alternatives in paper is critical. That said, too many choices can be overwhelming. While Via has a paper to meet your every need, it stops short of redundancy. Via is comprised of seven finishes and each has a palette of compatible colors. Fans of Mohawk papers are probably familiar with Mohawk's Vellum, Satin, and Tomohawk. These finishes have been added to the Via family to create a simple and comprehensive system.

Every day is Via Day

The wide range of options provides the versatility to meet any project's needs. Via is easy to use, easy to get, and easy on the budget. Whether your project involves four-color process, duotones, line art, or black and white images, Via has you covered. Our papers print beautifully, are easy to specify, and have incredible colors and textures. Mohawk Via's stable of papers is diverse but they're true workhorses.

Quality Control

Mohawk has always been linked with quality and value. Mohawk standards of excellence lead the industry in color, quality, formation, texture, opacity, smoothness, and printability.

The universal calendar AdamsMorioka designed for Mohawk Via is an example of the line's commitment to sustainable value—it's handsome, durable, and will never go out of date. Via's visual personality emerges in marketing vehicles so useful they won't be thrown away.

The same unifying message flows through the secondary product-extension logos, which define Via's finishes and create a distinct personality for each. These logos adopt a playful tone, are purposefully extremely varied, and mix Victorian and modern forms. None of the secondary logos is shown on its own. According to Adams, part of the brand-building process is to convey that all of these choices add up to one Mohawk Via. "The message is that Via is such a big family, it ought to be the only paper line a customer needs. Like your favorite pair of khakis, it can be dressed up or down depending on the kind of project you're doing."

Adams says the primary logo is now fixed, but the secondary logos are free to evolve according to their setting. For example, parts of the new Mohawk Via operator's manual employ imagery and forms related to Hawaii and the surfing world. While the primary Via logo remains constant, the secondary logos are adapted to reflect this theme.

"The message is that Via is such a big family, it ought to be the only paper line a customer needs. Like your favorite pair of khakis, it can be dressed up or down depending on the kind of project you're doing."

PRESERVING THE FUN FACTOR

AdamsMorioka's original Via identity had an attitude that was tongue-in-cheek, slightly kitschy, humorous, and irreverent. "While the first piece we designed didn't fall outside of the target demographic, we wanted to become more focused when addressing the line's new context," Adams relates. "Doing something frivolous now seemed inappropriate. Each piece [needed] to reflect usefulness and functionality." He describes the Via operator's manual and "fan deck" pieces, which provide extensive resources for designers working in the print medium, as "the most comprehensive paper promotions out there. They're sort of like *Pocket Pal* for the modern generation."

Another serious aim of the redesign was to advance Via's reputation as an ecofriendly paper. "One of the core values of Via is sustainability," Adams explains. "The target demographic for Via is younger, and these customers are committed to ecofriendly values." To charm these customers, AdamsMorioka sought to create marketing materials that won't be thrown away. Via's universal calendar is a prime example. This handsome "endless" calendar has earned a permanent place in many designers' workspaces.

Yet in keeping with Adams' philosophy that effective identity redesigns are always rooted in preserving equity, Via's new visual personality carries forward the most appealing and well-established quality of the company's character. The colorful new logo, which reflects the expanded range of colors Via offers, continues to send a playful message. When the logo is paired in marketing materials with offbeat patterns and whimsical imagery (squirrels holding spec cards, speech balloons asking "Dude, where's my paper?"), the visual personality that emerges stays true to the original Via's spirit of fun. The message: This is one paper line created expressly to spark the designer's imagination.

CREATIVE DIRECTOR: SEAN ADAMS
DESIGNERS: SEAN ADAMS, MONICA SCHLAUG
COPYWRITER: ADAMSMORIOKA

Inner-City Arts

Visualizing a Beacon for the Arts

DESIGN: PH.D, A DESIGN OFFICE
SANTA MONICA

WHEN INNER-CITY ARTS WAS FOUNDED IN 1989, it served a few hundred high-poverty children in temporary buildings on an elementary school campus in downtown Los Angeles. Four years later, the organization hired architect Michael Maltzan to renovate a former automotive paint shop on Skid Row for the school's permanent home. Maltzan brought in Michael Hodgson, principal and cofounder of Ph.D, to create signage for the building. The challenge was to come up with a design for the main building's identity that could be fabricated and installed for very little money.

The timing of the commission provided a unique opportunity. In the midst of the project, in January 1994, Los Angeles County suffered a massive earthquake that caused extensive structural damage throughout the metro area. "As I was driving through Santa Monica trying to figure how I could make a sign for the school with zero budget, I noticed several red-tagged apartment buildings with great old signs on them, such as Bali Hai and

The sign that Ph.D created for Inner-City Arts borrowed from Los Angeles' rich history of urban signage. Each letter was taken from a different context, and together they present a collage of type and scale that expresses the urban context, diversity, and creativity of the school.

The enormous scale of the letters allowed Hodgson both to honor the longstanding tradition of the neighborhood's fruit and vegetable wholesalers—which use large, painted murals to hawk their wares.

Bella Vista," recalls Hodgson. "I realized that if we could get hold of some of these old signs, we could put something together for Inner-City Arts where each letter was different. This would reflect the organization's urban roots and the varied creativity it supports."

Although this proved to be much more difficult than first imagined, Ph.D eventually sourced most of the needed type in a signage yard two hours east of Los Angeles. In addition, Hodgson was lucky enough to get several letters from the Henshey's Department Store, a former Santa Monica landmark, as it was being demolished.

THE ROAD TRAVELED

Though Inner-City Arts eventually installed the sign with great pride on its Kohler Street façade—where it remains to this day—they were initially resistant to updating or changing it's the school's logo, which was a line drawing of two children with an adult between them, all holding hands, enclosed in an oval. Designed by the school's founder and artistic director, Bob Bates, the former logo was based on figures used by an affiliated

Inner-City Arts' founder, Bob Bates, designed the original logo in 1989 based on figures used by an affiliated organization. Five years later, Ph.D redrew the figures to evoke the artistry of a child's paintbrush. They reset the type in Gill Sans and prioritized the school's name by placing it above the figures.
(Before: above, After: page 94)

organization that helped launch Inner-City Arts. Over the years, the logo was subtly modified, and the text was changed to reflect Inner-City Arts' independence. It was a DIY logo befitting an upstart organization with hands-on contact with children. Initially, Ph.D was asked to update the original artwork, now suffering from second- or third-generation decay. They redrew the figures in primary blue and softened the line to evoke the artistry of a child's paintbrush. They also reset the type in Gill Sans and prioritized the name of the organization by placing it above the figures with the tagline below.

As the school's programs and student body grew, Inner-City Arts purchased adjacent parcels and hired Maltzan to devise a master plan for expanding the campus into a compound of gleaming white modernist structures organized around open spaces and a courtyard. Wrapping around the end of a city block, two main entrances to the campus would remain on the side streets, with the school presenting a block-long white façade to 7th Street, a main thoroughfare through a troubled neighborhood.

VERY LARGE-SCALE GRAPHICS

With construction on the horizon, Inner-City Arts again approached Ph.D to design new signage for the campus. Maltzan was interested in "creating a graphic presence that would capture the transformative spirit of the school, and, importantly, could harness the dynamic and creative potential of this often-overlooked neighborhood, potential that can be seen if you look with open eyes." Inspired by the large-scale type on the architect's model of the campus and the signage for the architect's design for MoMA QNS, the Museum of Modern Art's temporary facility in Queens, New York, Hodgson designed a super-graphic for the blank façade, spelling out the organization's name in giant letters that would extend the full height of the campus' one- and two-story buildings, and reflect the rectilinear and trapezoidal shapes of Maltzan's buildings. Designed to span an entire city block when painted on the side of the building, the letters would present a legible, though semiabstract,

INNER-CITYARTS
INNER-CITYARTS

dance of forms to the street. The enormous scale of the letters allowed Hodgson both to honor the longstanding tradition of the neighborhood's fruit and vegetable wholesalers—which use large, painted murals to hawk their wares—and enable Inner-City Arts to stake a bold, yet tasteful claim for the school in a high poverty/high crime neighborhood. Hodgson carried the shapes and letters of the supergraphic through in signage on the interior of the campus, drawing on Maltzan's red and orange accents on the white buildings for his palette.

EXPANDING THE CAMPUS AND ITS IDENTITY

With the campus under construction, Inner-City Arts was also undergoing a major process of self-definition. It had grown from serving young children during the school day to also providing programs to more than 8,000 elementary, middle, and high school students. The school had added a sophisticated professional development program to train classroom teachers, and had become nationally recognized as a laboratory and research center for arts education. Its new campus would eventually serve 18,000 students and teachers.

Inner-City Arts realized it was time to present a new visual personality to not only represent the organization's complexity but also address the need for name recognition that would be essential to its growth. Kim Baer of KBDA, a communication design studio in L.A., was working with Inner-City Arts on its marketing. She persuaded the school to abandon its feel-good but generic logo with the argument that "it was indistinguishable from so many organizations that serve children and didn't convey anywhere near their sophistication." Hodgson concurred. "The it's-a-small-world-after-all message of the logo actually worked

In place of its original logo, Hodgson adapted the type he had developed for the building's supergraphic as the school's official mark. Not only would it imprint the organization's name in the minds of an expanded pool of stakeholders, it would also unite the image of the organization with its new campus.

Ph.D created a new type that reflected the trapezoidal and rectilinear forms of the new campus. The vibrant palette made Inner-City Arts' name leap off the bright white paper. The new logo presented the school's joyous, confident, creativity-affirming personality, while reflecting the architecture that proudly housed its endeavor.

against the school by reinforcing a negative stereotype that arts education is just playing with art supplies," he says. This was an impression Inner-City Arts was vigorously contradicting with research on its programs, which showed that education in the arts teaches vital skills that enhance not just students' creativity, but also their lives, academic achievement and sense of empowerment about their future.

In place of its original logo, Hodgson adapted as the school's official mark the type he had developed for the building's supergraphics. Not only would it imprint the organization's name in the minds of an expanded pool of stakeholders, it would also unite the image of the organization with its new campus. Cynthia Harnisch, Inner-City Arts CEO, saw this as critical. "Our identity is tied to our location in one of the city's poorest neighborhoods. Not

only are we one of the few arts education organizations to have a location, but for that location to be so spectacular is a powerful piece of who we are."

Hodgson built on Maltzan's vibrant palette of accent colors, injecting the forms of the supergraphic with a vitality that conveys the optimism and strength of the organization, while making Inner-City Arts' name leap out. The new logo presents the school's joyous, confident, creativity-affirming personality, while reflecting the architecture that proudly houses its endeavor.

"There are a lot of challenges around changing a logo," says Harnisch. "One is that so many people get involved in weighing in on the creative decisions that it can be diluted into something dull. What I loved about working with Mick was that he had a clear artistic vision and he was able to take a quantum leap forward. He stood

firm, and he was right. We see the payoff daily. When I give out my business card, people stop because it is so beautiful, and they always look at both sides. As an art school, we're very into the symbolism of color, and we're very interested in groups spiraling upward. Red exemplifies the heart and passion. Yellow represents the intellect and wisdom. Orange is the perfect blend of both. The new logo represents exactly where we want to stand in the world as a creative arts center. People tell me now that when they see orange, they think of us."

CREATIVE DIRECTOR: MICHAEL HODGSON
DESIGNERS: MICHAEL HODGSON, KEITH KNEUVEN
PROJECT MANAGERS: SELENE GLADSTONE, RANDY WALKER
ARCHITECT: MICHAEL MALTZAN & ASSOCIATES
PHOTOGRAPHS: PAGES 90, 95. IWAN BAAN, WWW.IWAN.COM

INNER-CITYARTS

INNER-CITYARTS

The Mark Taper Center **Inner-City Arts**
720 Kohler Street | Los Angeles CA 90021

Address Service Requested

CYNTHIA S. HARNISCH   PRESIDENT AND CEO
cynthia@inner-cityarts.org | 213 627 9621 | FAX 213 627 6469

720 Kohler Street | Los Angeles CA 90021 | www.inner-cityarts.org

720 Kohler Street | Los Angeles CA 90021 | **213.627.9621** | fax 213.627.6469 | www.inner-cityarts.org

WUMB Boston

Can You Hear Me Now?

DESIGN: MINELLI INC.
BOSTON

WUMB RADIO OF BOSTON, MASSACHUSETTS, HAS LONG BEEN REGARDED AS ONE OF THE COUNTRY'S PREMIER public radio stations for folk and acoustical music, but the number of listeners was falling. To help combat that, the station applied for and received a grant from the Corporation for Public Broadcasting intended to help increase awareness of its programming.

WUMB executives realized its reputation as the best source for folk and acoustic music limited its appeal. Moreover, the perception was untrue. WUMB offered much more, but in public radio it is risky to alienate your most loyal audience. They are the ones who donate most generously and regularly. Pat Montieth, station manager at WUMB, says this did not prevent the station from making the leap.

"Many die-hard folk fans have expressed that the new logo moves us too far away from being clearly identified as a folk music station. This is not a problem for us. These are the same listeners who generally have been vocal—about any changes we have made over the years."

PERCEPTION GAP

In fact, WUMB's research told them that those vocal listeners were not the only ones with a strong opinion: existing audiences had broader tastes. The preexisting identity simply led to preconceptions that kept newcomers from even considering WUMB. To increase public awareness and new audiences, that new station identity needed to express the diversity of its programming. Thus, the logo was completely redesigned by Minelli Inc. of Boston. Those limiting acoustic guitars were purged. Only the call letters remained.

"The new logo has moved WUMB away from being thought of as just a radio station for aging hippies. There is no longer a preconceived notion in the minds of potential listeners about what they think we must sound like," says Montieth.

Before (top left): WUMB's folksy old logo belied the station's diverse programming and restricted its appeal.
After (bottom left): Minelli Inc.'s no-strings version connects with a broader audience on a new abstract frequency. No aging hippies were harmed in the testing of this new logo.

"The new identity has broader appeal, is bolder, and more contemporary. Pat Montieth believes the improved audience numbers are attributable to the new design," notes Trisha Leavitt of Minelli.

In fact, Montieth says the recent 26 percent audience increase is attributed, in part, to the redesign: "With our old guitars logo and 'Folk Radio' moniker, potential new listeners were influenced by what they expected to hear. The simple, contemporary design of the new logo—combined with our new tagline—invites an open-mindedness we've never before enjoyed."

CREATIVE DIRECTOR: MARK MINELLI
ART DIRECTOR: TRISHA LEAVITT, YUKO INAGAKI
DESIGNERS: TRISHA LEAVITT, YUKO INAGAKI, ALEX FRIEND
RESEARCH AND STRATEGY: MARK RUCKMAN, EMILY PAISNER

Brooklyn Botanic Garden

Planting a Good Idea

DESIGN: CARBONE SMOLAN
NEW YORK

100

BROOKLYN BOTANIC GARDEN IS A TRANQUIL 52-ACRE URBAN OASIS. Composed of exquisite and historic specialty gardens, it's also committed to education, outreach, and scientific research. It's a trusted source of information on horticulture and botany and an authoritative voice for environmental protection and plant conservation.

Yet for much of its history, Brooklyn Botanic Garden's identity had languished in the shade, says Ken Carbone. "When we were called on to develop a new identity for Brooklyn Botanic, we knew right away we needed to demonstrate a sense of high esteem."

"Working with the curators and botanists at the garden, we were struck by their deep emotional connection with botany and the natural world," Carbone recalls. "This project warranted a visual symbol, and the garden's director was enthusiastic about finding one with a sense of growth. They also felt the need to send a new message to their audience, especially because they were about to embark on significant changes at the garden that would mean fund raising from an expanded base of benefactors. One of our ideas was to create a dynamic symbol that isn't contained within a shape to reflect the growth and dynamism of the organization."

There wasn't much equity in the existing logo. Yet while the old mark was "dated, visually congested, and clumsy," (in Carbone's words), it did get one thing right in its visual language: Brooklyn Botanic Garden is about plants.

PLANTS AND SYMBOLS

So the new identity should include an image of a plant. But what sort of plant? Confronting this question, Carbone recalls, was a critical moment in the process.

"It's always difficult to create a symbol that's distinctive and strong," he says. "In this case, we had to be careful to come up with a symbol for

Before (bottom left): Brooklyn Botanic Garden's previous logo was dated, visually congested, and clumsy. **After (top left):** Carbone Smolan's new identity retains some equity—the botanical concept—from the original, but delivers it with greater elegance. The system is designed so the symbol and typography can be used separately or together with equal success.
Opposite: In addition to being designed for scalability, the new symbol can be interpreted in a variety of ways, with and without color.

'every' plant, not something that could be identified as a specific plant. The symbol had to say 'flora.'" After all, the garden has more than 11,000 different varieties. And the symbol had to send its message at all sizes and in a variety of media. All of this suggested a measure of abstraction would be desirable.

Carbone Smolan's design solution achieves the desired symbolic elegance, but its value goes deeper. "We decided to 'unbundle' the mark from the type so they could be used separately or together," Carbone says. The strategy multiplies the versatility of the identity system, allowing it to serve in different business roles (marketing, advertising, fund raising) and across formats (web, print, stationery). The system takes advantage of the intuitive nature of a great symbol, working equally well with color and without. As Carbone puts it, "You *identify* a mark more than you *read* it."

The designers also contributed a new tagline: "Where plants come to life." Carbone explains: "This is much a part of what we do. A branding system often needs an effective tagline, and it shouldn't be an afterthought."

PRINCIPAL: KEN CARBONE
DESIGN DIRECTOR: CARLA MILLER
DESIGNER: DOMINICK RICCI
ADMINISTRATIVE: SAMANTHA WOODS

Reflections of Life

JAIPUɼ

HAND-KNOTTED WOOL AND SILK RUG FROM THE CONCOURSE COLLECTION
JAIPURRUGS.COM 888 676 7330 HIGH POINT ATLANTA LAS VEGAS NEW DELHI

Jaipur
Nice Rug!

DESIGN: GRANT DESIGN COLLABORATIVE
ATLANTA

JAIPUR IS A TEXTILE AND FURNITURE DESIGN COMPANY that has been around for a century based in the city of the same name—Jaipur, India. Jaipur's U.S. headquarters are based in Atlanta, Georgia, where Grant Design Collaborative is also based. Founder Bill Grant recalls, "The CEO and her father—the company owner, who was visiting from India—came to hear me address the ASID (American Society of Interior Designers) talk in Atlanta. A few weeks later, the CEO called me and asked if we'd be interested in doing some rug designs for them.

"Jaipur does beautiful hand-knotted wool and silk rugs based on antique Persian patterns. But the client had a notion to do more modern and contemporary rugs for the American consumer," says Grant. "She wanted to move the brand forward in many ways."

After Grant and team began working with Jaipur, they soon learned the CEO wanted to get into accessories and furniture and other things. "We pointed out that there were some issues with the existing logo," said Grant. "So she hired us to redo their brand, from strategy to identity."

JAIPUR
R U G S ,   I N C .

JAIPUR

Before (top): For one thing, Jaipur makes more than rugs; the previous construction was limiting.
After (bottom): The new logotype is a model of restraint allowing for complexity (and delight) in application with things like die-cut covers. Grant took away the symbol and the word *rug* so "when the brand evolve in the future, we don't have to go back and change the logo," says Bill Grant.

The logotype is simple but complexity is revealed in its application. Their product catalog, for example, has a die cut in the logo on the front of the cover and the back cover is a die cut *R*, the exact reverse of the *J* letterform. The contemporary look was created to appeal to American audiences.

"The design in this category is generally tired—you know, the typical palm trees and pineapples—so we tried a more modern graphic sensibility to play outdoor themes such as corals, bear tracks, and other fun things. So the work we did for Jaipur is more than just an identity—it is a symbol of what we're doing for the company, moving them into the future," Grant explains.

His company believes long-term commitments from clients are a perfect fit for his firm. Jaipur, for example, contracted with Grant Design Collaborative for eighteen months to redo the identity and redo the rug collections. Like most, their process starts with discovery: look at their market—rugs, interior furnishings; competitive analysis to see what's available in that

category. But Grant's people dig deeper, seeking to identify the unmet wants and needs of the consumers. They assessed Jaipur's brand awareness by talking to sales people, customers, suppliers, and big retailers from Crate and Barrel to mom-and-pop furniture dealers.

This deep research led to a revelation. They found out that Jaipur was revered for its color and color combinations—something they weren't even celebrating. Grant thus created a new color palette for them using bright, vibrant colors—all based on Indian spices.

"The palette," adds Grant, "honors heritage and origins of Jaipur, which is one of the decorative capitals of India. We incorporated more contemporary materials but avoided clichés. With that nod to heritage, we aimed for the future, redoing their logo, identity, and catalogs."

Grant has one secret weapon: "Road Mapping." After the discovery phase concludes (which it never really does), the team begins building a brand road map for every client. You can think of it like a scrapbook into which relevant information and work is clipped and pasted. As of today, the

Jaipur road map document is ninety pages and growing. In it the client will find strategy and analysis, research findings and brand benchmarks. There's also a section on shifting consumer values and tastes—what they looked for in the past, what they are currently looking for, what they might value tomorrow. Throughout the project, the team is constantly seeing ways to help their client customize their product to suit more individual wants and needs.

Indian Spice. As far as the company's Indian heritage, the name *Jaipur* is a city in India famed for its crafts and artisans. Rather than create some clichéd mark or symbol, Grant lets the word stand alone and pays homage to India with colors inspired by commonly used Indian spices such as cumin and cardamom.

As far as messaging, Grant boils their values down to three elements. He explains, "Jaipur holds three brand virtues: the head, the heart, and the hand. First, it's a thoughtful company, a smart company. Second, they treat their people well (many of village women weave at home so they do not have to go to industrial centers and leave behind their way of life). Finally, the hand represents the fact that most of their products are made by hand, which is why the rugs are so valuable as heirlooms. Everything kind of centers around these three values."

The goal of all this effort is to grow Jaipur by taking them from their traditional client base—mom-and-pop rug dealers—and take them to architects and dealers for hospitality, healthcare, and retail rugs.

Back to the identity, it is simple. The Jaipur logotype reverses out of the box that may or may not be in color. The word *rug* was eliminated from the original identity, as was a dated Persian symbol.

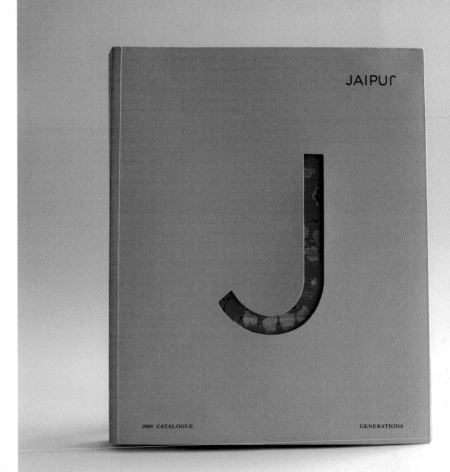

"I'm really not a big fan of marks or symbols because most of the time they end up backing a client into a corner," Grant says. "When people see visuals, they see peculiar things, or it's hard for them to see beyond that. The previous symbol really represented their past. We took the word *rug* and the symbol away so when the brand becomes something else in the future, we don't have to go back and change the logo."

As far as heritage and equity, "Indian" is implied because Jaipur is a city in India and Indian spices such as cumin, cardamom, and chili inspired all the colors. That's it. Beautiful and simple.

ALL CREATIVE AND COPY:
GRANT DESIGN COLLABORATIVE

DevelopMentor
Cleared for Takeoff

LAUNCHED IN 1993, DEVELOPMENTOR IS A COMPANY THAT DEVELOPS, TRAINS, AND MENTORS people who develop and write software. Its founder, Mike Abercrombie, is a great proponent of the value of graphic design. He is also extremely loyal: he hired Santa Monica–based Ph.D the year he started his company to design its first logo, and he still works with them today. "I go to them and they get it," says Abercrombie. "There is a lot to be said for longevity."

Over the years, Ph.D has created four different versions of the DevelopMentor identity. The first update in 1998 reflected the forming of five separate departments within the company and a new direction the client was heading in. When that direction turned out to be a dead end in 2003, that version of the identity died, too, and the department logos were retired, but the basic logotype remained. The current design was done in 2009. "Every iteration was appropriate for its time," says Abercrombie."

Before (above top): DevelopMentor's original logotype needed to be refined as the company expanded and added departments.
Before (above 2nd from top): DevelopMentor's earlier paper airplane mark, with its slender lowercase type, had to make an early landing.
After (above 3, 4 & 5): Ph.D.'s 2009 upgrade features Knockout capitals and a beefier plane, now shown during takeoff.

Abercrombie had bought another company and was merging them to create an entity with a much larger scope of services, so an update to the identity was needed to better reflect the new course his business was heading and the new people (trainers, mentors, consultants) he had hired to get them there. In short, he was moving, in his words, "from attire fitting for a backyard Sunday barbecue to attire more fitting for a black-tie dinner." Never ones to walk away from good work or the chance to buy a new whistle, the blokes at Ph.D commenced tailoring DevelopMentor's new formal dinner suit.

Abercrombie's background is important to this discussion. Before entering the world of IT, he worked in the music industry. Cutting edge was his middle name. He was ahead of the curve with the Internet. How on earth does one get the URL "www.develop.com," unless they were standing in line the night before the first URL was sold? Abercrombie prides himself on that but knows trends are fickle friends. That is why he believes so much in the power of design to tell the story. And because stories change, design must, too.

"Not long ago, a friend sent me a copy of a 1975 J.C. Penney's catalog," recalls Abercrombie. "And I was looking at the clothing in that thing and I thought, 'what were we thinking?!' Well, I think of identity as something one

wears. Would you where your 1975 corduroy jacket to a business meeting? Not if you wanted to be taken seriously. You would change it. And we have changed our identity, carefully, to reflect the maturation and evolution of our people and our market position."

The most recent iteration is designed to help introduce Develop-Mentor to a whole new upper echelon of corporations. Abercrombie calls the logo and logotype the company "handshake"—and that hand is attached to the people who work there. He wanted it to be bolder (the font is Knockout, and it is bolder) and more muscular. The plane got "bigger engines" and more detail, going from a Cessna to a B-52 paper airplane. Robust.

"I am not so much worried that our customers like it, but this is our handshake and our look," Abercrombie says. "I want to be assured that it really reflects the people here and that they like it, that it represents them. I think the consensus here is that it does."

Oh. And why the paper airplane? First, it dates back to the beginning of the company history. Here was the Ph.D rationale that sold Abercrombie:

"When you were a child, did you ever try to make a paper airplane? Do you remember how many times you were unsuccessful? Do you recall that nine of ten of your paper airplanes, when launched, nosed dived straight away into the ground? Then came that magical moment, the special time when one, surprising, delightful, stunning paper airplane crafted with your own young hands flew far and straight and high forever. Well, DevelopMentor helps others be that one."

CREATIVE DIRECTOR: MICHAEL HODGSON
DESIGNERS: MICHAEL HODGSON, DERRICK SCHULTZ, ALICE JOO

TITANS *of* DESIGN

FRANK GEHRY / PHILIPPE STARCK / JOHN LAUTNER / J MAYS

Los Angeles Times Magazine

OCTOBER 05, 2008

CASE STUDY

LA [magazine]

Just Like I Pictured It

DESIGNER: RIP GEORGES
LOS ANGELES

RIP GEORGES IS REGARDED AS ONE OF THE NATION'S PREEMINENT publication and fashion advertising designers. He is also a life-long friend of mine. My association with him began in the early 1970s when Georges was doing postgraduate work at the same school, Brighton College of Art, where he won my friendship while he stole my girlfriend. I eventually followed Rip to Los Angeles. He gave me my first job here, helping me get started as I established myself in Los Angeles.

Here, we discuss two great examples of brand evolution at two famous brands: the former *Los Angeles Times Magazine*, where Georges now serves as creative director, and Brooks Brothers, where he served as consulting creative director in the late '90s as well as getting a few monogrammed shirts made.

1.   2.

3.   4.

Changes in ownership at the Tribune Company—also owners of the *Chicago Tribute*, the *Baltimore Sun*, and the *Orlando Sentinel*—led to changes in editorial content. That meant cost cutting. Since the magazine had never been profitable, it was a natural for the

Before (below): The venerable *Los Angeles Times Magazine* had many fans during its 35-year run. But the magazine's soaring costs and declining revenues forced it into retirement.
After (top left): Rip Georges decided the new magazine had to be more fashionable, more design oriented, and bolder. The famed iconoclast font designer Jim Parkinson of Oakland, California, drew the new logotype.

chopping block. But the magazine also had earned its fans after a 35-year run. So, after closing it down for a short time, the powers that be decided to relaunch it and change its focus. Rather than a general interest and news magazine, the focus would be on style: fashion, food, home, garden, and (the inevitable) celebrity—this is Los Angeles!

"Those things had always been a part of the former magazine," says Georges. "But they were not its focus. In this market, they are an obvious place to focus and try to recapture the imagination of readers. Importantly, the magazine would no longer be controlled by the newsroom."

Thus, the Tribune Corporation turned it over to people with long experience in magazine design and editorial. People like Georges. The first thing the new team did was rename the magazine. It had been long called any number of names, including *City*, *Los Angeles Times Magazine*, *LA Times Magazine*, and *LA Times Sunday Magazine*. The LA abbreviation was the obvious shorthand. It became the name.

Next, Georges, known for being a bit of a type geek, hired one of the leading font designers in the world, Jim Parkinson, an "Oakland hippie" whose credits include *Newsweek*, *Rolling Stone*, *San Francisco Examiner*, and *Esquire*. He had also modified the typeface of *LA Times* at one point. It was upon that design that the new *LA* magazine typeface was based. Georges and Parkinson had collaborated before, on *In Style* magazine.

Even with all this heritage, equity, in the name, the acronym, past versions of the LA Times typeface, the new visual personality has a lot more edge, funk, street to it. In fact, primary inspiration came from Mr. Cartoon, a famous LA tattoo artist who works out of studio in downtown LA.

"I loved this guy's work. It is East LA, very prison tat," says Georges. "So we took the *LA* monogram and pushed, giving it block letters, a more stylize look, and more street personality. The space between *L* and *A* was a natural place for a big, bold graphic. We made it a swoosh. I told all of my younger colleagues that they should all get this tattooed on the nape of their necks."

Does Rip Georges have it tattooed on the nape of his neck? "Not yet. After all these years telling my children not to get tattoos, now I might have to eat my words," he says.

The success of this work is not just the logotype. It is in the art direction of the magazine; its original artwork and spare design. The proof of success of any magazine is proven over the course of a long life. George and *LA* magazine have had a nice start in a difficult economy, especially for the publication business. Rip Georges is optimistic about the future of LA—the magazine and the city.

CREATIVE DIRECTOR AND DESIGN DIRECTOR:
RIP GEORGES
LOGO DESIGNERS: JIM PARKINSON,
RIP GEORGES
LOGO FINAL RENDERING: JIM PARKINSON

Prison Tat. Rip Georges claims some inspiration by famed LA tattoo artist Mr. Cartoon. The new LA logo is a reflection of that—a big, phat, street graphic. LA County jail inmates did not participate in focus group research—yet.

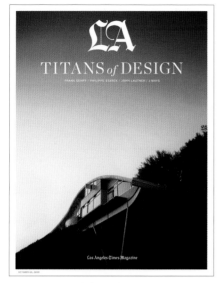

TITANS *of* DESIGN

FRANK GEHRY / PHILIPPE STARCK / JOHN LAUTNER / J MAYS

Los Angeles Times Magazine

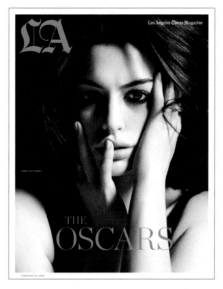

THE OSCARS

Los Angeles Times Magazine

Los Angeles Times Magazine

TASTEMAKERS

Abbie
Cornish
Shines
Bright

by LESLIE GORNSTEIN

photographs by
RUVEN AFANADOR

Los Angeles Times Magazine

Los Angeles Times Magazine

Divine
MADNESS
The BEST *of* FALL FASHION
by LORI GOLDSTEIN

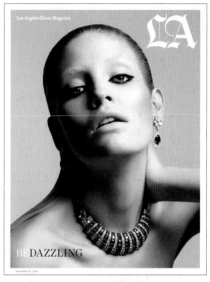

Los Angeles Times Magazine

BE DAZZLING

Los Angeles Times Magazine

FINE FEATHERED FASHION / *The* PROPHESS *of and the* POM QUEEN / *VIVA the* LAKERS

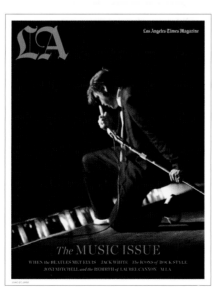

Los Angeles Times Magazine

The MUSIC ISSUE

WHEN *the* BEATLES MET ELVIS / JACK WHITE / *The* ICONS *of* ROCK STYLE
JONI MITCHELL *and the* REBIRTH *of* LAUREL CANYON / M.I.A.

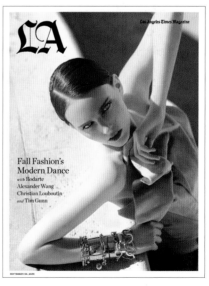

Los Angeles Times Magazine

Fall Fashion's
Modern Dance
with
Rodarte
Alexander Wang
Christian Louboutin
and Tim Gunn

BROOKS BROTHERS

RIP GEORGES' WORK FOR BROOKS Brothers in 1998 and 1999 is an equally distinguished example of identity evolution.

A millennium was ending, and Brooks Brothers, who had been around for 180 years of it, was facing a problem common to well-established brands of a conservative nature: their buyers, too, were old, conservative, and established—and getting older. They needed to attract a new crop of dapper dudes.

But how do you refresh your brand without driving away the conservative buyer? How do you get the old dudes and the young dudes to shop at the same place? The company had to find the sweet spot between dignity and stodginess. It had to welcome new customers without looking desperate.

The bold Bodoni preexisting Georges' involvement was stodgy. It needed to go. Georges made his case for change to the Brooks Brothers script through careful research. Combing through the company archives in Washington, D.C., Georges saw many subtle changes to the brand over the years. "I saw enough variation that I could make my case," recalls Georges. "And I was very interested in the old monograms and typestyles with more truncated script. They reminded me of some of the past work for *Esquire*."

Georges created a new Brooks Brothers script with a clearer baseline, truncating the alphabet by lopping off the bottom of the letter *B*. He then created a monogram double *B* that could be used in advertising. "My one disappointment is that the monogram has more or less been abandoned," says Georges. "But I see the script as we designed it all the time, and that is very gratifying."

All good things will come to pass: in art, fashion, and blueblood brands like Brooks Brothers.

CREATIVE DIRECTOR AND DESIGN DIRECTOR:
RIP GEORGES, RIP GEORGES + ASSOCIATES (RGA)
LOGO DESIGN: TOM CARNASE, RIP GEORGES
LOGO FINAL RENDERING: TOM CARNASE

BROOKS BROTHERS

Before (above): Like all great fashion brands, when your past becomes your present, you might not be attracting new buyers. There was nothing wrong with the old logotype, per se, but it did not resonate with new, fashionable buyers. Georges made it a monogram.
After (below): George's 1998 makeover for Brooks Brothers was more than a just logo redesign; it was a new approach to communicating the Brooks Brothers brand story that appealed to new audiences and gave the iconic brand new life and buyers.

Hartford Stage
Enter Stage Right

DESIGN: CARBONE SMOLAN
NEW YORK

114

KEN CARBONE SOMETIMES FEELS LIKE HE'S TALKING HIMSELF OUT OF BUSINESS when clients come to his New York studio for a logo redesign. "If a logo has equity, recognition, or a legacy, I have to ask: 'Why change?'" he says. "Change is difficult under the best circumstances, so the reasons for a redesign have to be sound."

To challenge his clients to consider the "why" question in depth, Carbone borrows a trick from Socrates, another fellow who talked himself out of business. "We approach clients with the assumption that their reasons for changing are unclear," he says.

Asking the "why" question is step 1 in Carbone Smolan's process for undertaking an identity revamp, and for good reason. An identity redesign is a tremendous job, and a client needs a clearly expressed, honestly motivated will to carry it through. The systematic changes involved in creating and implementing a new logo are wide-ranging and can be expensive—a fact that's sometimes not immediately evident to clients.

HARTFORD · STAGE

Before (top): The existing Hartford Stage logo was perfunctory and industrial—not a symbol of an energetic and much-admired performing arts organization.

After (bottom and opposite): Carbone Smolan's new identity for Hartford Stage envisions letter-forms as "a colorful cast of characters on a small, square stage."

"The logo to me is really the tip of the iceberg," Carbone says. "It's everything *under* it that's really important. Sometimes a logo can survive, but just needs to be packaged better. I'm not convinced a logo always has to change unless it's damaging to the company's reputation, sending the wrong signals, or doesn't hold up technically over the major channels of distribution. Obviously, if you're Enron or Blackwater, you have to do something."

WHEN THE MARK IS OFF THE MARK

Then there's Hartford stage, a popular and highly regarded regional theater in Hartford, Connecticut. Its logo wasn't exactly damaging its reputation, but

the drab and rather perfunctory mark wasn't doing it any good, either. Carbone Smolan filed it under "sending the wrong signals."

"The existing logo completely contradicted the energetic reality of this theater and the vision of its artistic director," Carbone explains. "The type treatment was industrial—it wasn't sending the message that this is a lively arts institution." The task of exploring a new identity happened to coincide with the fortieth anniversary of the theater's founding, providing an ideal opportunity to encourage new interest and support from the theater's membership.

After establishing that a new logo would be necessary, Carbone Smolan conducted a series of high-level meetings involving one-on-one interviews with board members and others. This consensus-building and clarification is step 2 in their process. "About twelve years ago, we began developing techniques for helping organizations understand their identity," Carbone says, noting that while the process—called Greenlighting—is proprietary, it's enough to know it's based on the client's answers to two questions: 1) Who are you today? 2) Who do you need to be tomorrow to grow your organization? Discussions and debates among stakeholders within the client reveal the attributes in need of expression, the personality of the company—the soul, which the new identity will embody.

To capture the spirit of the Hartford Stage, the designers attended performances and rehearsals. And the effort paid off, as concepts inspired by the world of theater proved crucial in the final design solution. Creating an icon or symbol wasn't necessary, because the name of the theater has such strong recognition, Carbone says. "We found we could pull from the language of the theater and carry that voice forward in a number of ways."

A true logotype, the typographically driven final design also manages to function as a symbol in print, web, and display applications. The letters in the mark were envisioned, in Carbone's words, as a "colorful cast of characters on a small, square stage." To drive the point home, the letters in the name are split up and stacked, compressing the logo and allowing the ensemble of upper- and lowercase letterforms to work its playful magic. The eye delights in exploring this unexpected arrangement, tracing out surprising connections in hidden words—*art*, *forge*, *roar*—which seem to hold the

secret of the place. A wide range of color treatments provides distinction and versatility.

"We also proposed a tagline, 'all the world's,' for use on stationery," Carbone adds. The cleverly adapted quote from Shakespeare's *As You Like It* is perfectly suited to an established and esteemed theater. At the same time, the new Hartford Stage identity is what Carbone feels every effective logo must be: "A flexible way to send a broader message to the wide world."

PRINCIPAL: KEN CARBONE
DESIGN DIRECTOR: CARLA MILLER
DESIGNER: MELANIE WIESENTHAL
PROJECT MANAGER: RACHEL SIMMONS

Fort Mason Center
Mission Accomplished

DESIGN: CHEN DESIGN ASSOCIATES
SAN FRANCISCO

"REDESIGNING A LOGO ISN'T ALWAYS AS SIMPLE AS FINDING *THE* VOICE OF THE CLIENT," says Josh Chen, principal of Chen Design Associates (CDA). "A client can have many voices. An important part of the design process is helping the client rationalize them all." For Chen, an identity redesign is about making sure all the voices get heard—even the unexpected ones.

Fort Mason Center is a popular waterfront destination in San Francisco. The massive retired military base hosts more than 15,000 events each year, in addition to hosting two dozen nonprofit resident organizations on its 13 acres (5.2 hectares). Exhibits, fairs, lectures, festivals, performances, and symposia, as well as classes and workshops for all ages and interests, are held in its Mission Revival rental buildings, grounds, and piers.

The center attracts 1.6 million Bay Area residents annually. Reflecting all of these perspectives—picking out all of the voices in this tremendous choir—was the formidable task that fell to CDA when they were asked to redesign Fort Mason Center's identity.

Before (top): Sure, it was simple, but it was also a dated piece of a larger city park's design system that communicated little about the center as resource and destination. Nor did it accommodate the voices of center tenants.

After (bottom): CDA gave the center's new identity a sense of place by celebrating the unique architecture of the center and they built-in flexibility that gave center tenants room to express their own voice as well.

HORSE AND CART

Curiously, the process didn't begin with an identity at all. It began with a website revamp—one that CDA wasn't even involved with.

Though self-sufficient in day-to-day operating expenses, the center relies on outside sources to fund capital improvements and special projects. Recognizing that mounting a capital campaign to upgrade its facilities and improve access to public transportation would require a new website, the center contracted with a local firm. But as the site grew ready for its unveiling, center managers realized they couldn't just plop their old logo—an extension of a dated city Parks and Recreation Department mark—into the new online setting.

Enter CDA. With a frank admission that "Fort Mason Center has neglected to provide a cohesive and compelling organizational identity," facility managers prepared a detailed design brief outlining requirements and goals for a new identity system. It was a call to action that recognized, in the words of Josh Chen, that "it was time for the center to stand on its own."

A SENSE OF PLACE, WITH AND WITHOUT ART

Fort Mason Center's existing identity didn't offer much to work from. But where others might have seen a limitation and a vacuum, CDA saw an opportunity, a space for creative play. They had the freedom to find the voices of the complex. "The client really looked to us to discover what makes Fort Mason Center stand out as a community resource," recalls CDA's lead designer Max Spector. "They had the place, and they looked to us for a logo that would create a sense of that place."

A key reason CDA was chosen for the redesign was the firm's acclaimed mastery of typography. Type was critical, because the identity system had to work both with and without pictorial elements. Organizations renting space at the center produce their own promotional materials, and these materials would not always accommodate the full logo with both type and symbol. In addition, signage requirements meant that directional and identifying type would often have to stand on its own (see "Fort Mason Center: Logo Design Requirements," page 119). The type not only had to blend many voices—it had to speak many languages.

"One of the things impressed upon us early was the importance of our typographic solution," says Chen. "This was one reason we presented such a wide range of type treatments. The client team was new to working together, and going through the process of choosing allowed them to discover who they are and explore all that the identity needed to accomplish."

Initial presentations by CDA included eleven distinct identities, grouped in families with associated type. As is often the case when working with a non-profit organization, developing consensus was a major part of the job. "Getting everyone to buy in is often the most difficult and challenging aspect of a redesign," Chen remarks. "From the time we made our initial presentation, the client team had strong responses; different members had different personal favorites." But by closely comparing the treatments against their list of needs, the team and CDA steadily coalesced, assembling in the end a single "toolbox" that would satisfy all requirements.

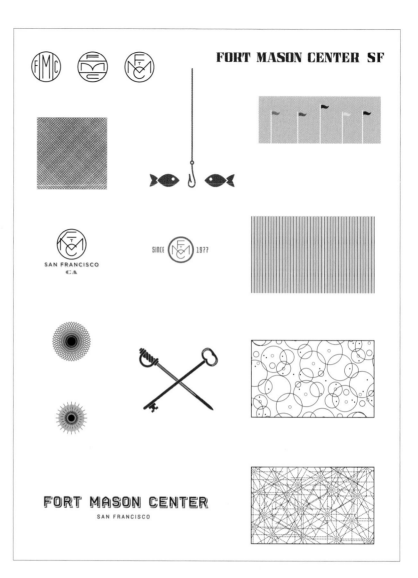

A MULTIDIMENSIONAL SYSTEM

The chosen solution incorporates several elements—image/symbol, custom type, general-purpose text and display type, and an associated monogram-type symbol. The imagery representing Fort Mason buildings resonates with the history of the former naval base, yet without being overtly military. The building image, true to the center's architectural style, is paired with atmospheric custom type to form the complete logo. As desired, the logo's distinctive custom type is capable of conveying a sense of place by itself.

The FMC circle "monogram" was adopted from one of the early directions presented to the client, but it works superbly with the logo in terms of sensibility, style, and again the ability to reflect historical and current-day dimensions of the center.

FORT MASON CENTER:
LOGO DESIGN REQUIREMENTS

Finally, the commercial typefaces Sentinel (serif) and Knockout (sans serif), both from Hoefler & Frere-Jones, complete the basic identity elements.

ONGOING ADAPTATION

First applied in mid-2009, the toolkit is still in its formative stages. CDA expects to continue developing it for some time to come. But the system's unique balance of consistency and flexibility—its blended gesture toward both the center's history and its 21st-century mission—is already yielding benefits, says Spector. "It's exciting to see that a logo can serve many needs without going to the lowest common denominator. That is especially gratifying for us."

CREATIVE DIRECTOR, ART DIRECTOR:
JOSHUA C. CHEN
DESIGN DIRECTOR: LAURIE CARRIGAN
DESIGNER, ILLUSTRATOR: MAX SPECTOR

- COLOR PALETTE must reproduce consistently in multiple color spaces: RGB, CMYK, PMS
- Identity symbol must work seamlessly with the name *Fort Mason Center* when typeset
- Identity must work vertically, horizontally, flush left or right and centered. Two different configurations, vertical and horizontal are welcome.
- Identity must work printed large (banners, billboards), as well as miniscule (as a sponsor footnoted on a postcard).
- Typeface family must accommodate three categories:
  1) printed reading text for newsletters and annual reports
  2) display and directional text, for banners and signage
  3) symbol paired with typeset name of *Fort Mason Center*
- Typeface family must be versatile in order to promote
  1) upscale development events
  2) casual family/children's events
  3) general marketing usage
- Recommendation for Web text typeface that relates to above typeface family

Invigorating Seaweed CONDITIONER

Smoothes ALL HAIR TYPES

DEEPLY NOURISHING AVOCADO OIL IS COMBINED WITH A
TONING HERBAL INFUSION OF SEAWEED AND ROSEMARY
AND ESSENTIAL OILS OF LEMON AND LAVENDER TO
LEAVE HAIR SOFT AND SMOOTH

APPLY TO DAMP HAIR AND WORK THROUGH EVENLY
LEAVE FOR A FEW MINUTES BEFORE RINSING

MADE IN ENGLAND
TIC FRAGRANCES OR COLOURS • NO PARABENS • WE

Invigorating Seaweed SHAMPOO

Gently cleanses ALL HAIR TYPES

A MINERAL RICH TONIC WITH AN INFUSION OF
SEAWEED COMBINED WITH GENTLE PLANT BASED
CLEANSERS AND FRESH SCENTED ROSEMARY

WET HAIR WITH WARM WATER, APPLY SHAMPOO
SPARINGLY AND WORK INTO A RICH LATHER
RINSE THOROUGHLY AND REPEAT AS NECESSARY

MADE IN ENGLAND
TIC FRAGRANCES OR COLOURS • NO PARABENS • NO SILICONES

Neal's Yard Remedies

Got Some Bottle?

DESIGN: ABOUD CREATIVE
LONDON

LED BY ALAN ABOUD, ABOUD CREATIVE has been working with Neal's Yard Remedies for more than three years. The firm's role has been far-reaching, helping the organic cosmetic maker develop and refine its entire visual presentation, including packaging, point of purchase, advertising, and sales collateral. Neal's Yard Remedies regards itself as a pioneer in natural remedies, skin and body care. In 1981, it opened its first shop in London, on Neal's Yard Alley in Covent Garden between Short Gardens and Monmouth Street.

The area, dotted with several other health-food cafés and new-age boutiques, was an early haven of the upstart natural-lifestyle business, and Neal's took the mindset of a kind neighbor to its work: the stated goal of company founders was to bring the "expertise of the apothecary and our holistic approach to health and beauty to local people and their communities." Since these halcyon communal beginnings, Neal's Yard has grown to become a beauty brand known and respected around the world. It has many stores throughout the United Kingdom, as well in the U.S. and Japan.

Under the new ownership of Peter Kindersley, it was determined that the brand needed a lift, something to help it stand out in the ever-crowded market for natural and organic health and beauty products. Aboud tightened, lightened, and highlighted the visual system, from packaging to advertising.

According to Alan Aboud, "We created an *evolved* visual aesthetic that's natural and contemporary, with an easy, confident style. It reaffirms the brand's quality and the authenticity of all-natural ingredients." The changes are subtle but the effect is dramatic.

The iconic blue bottle, of course, remained. And the simple, straightforward type style remained. But the design has more clarity and purpose. It doesn't just look folksy and quaint—it informs and guides the consumer. Like the former flower children of Covent Garden now raising families on Notting Hill, the brand has grown up.

"We discovered people love the products but had trouble reading the labels. If you weren't careful, you'd buy the wrong thing—because the typography was so miniscule, and the

Good Morning. Without touching the Neal's Yard iconic bottle, Aboud's redesign took what was once merely a quaint type treatment and gave it clarity and purpose—important when you don't want to mistake your favorite laxative for your Neal's Yard hair conditioner one bleary-eyed morning.

DESIGN DIRECTOR, CREATIVE DIRECTOR, DESIGNER: ALAN ABOUD

color system they had did not really help," Aboud says. "What we did basically was create a color system and very simple typography that was more legible from a greater distance. We've had a few tweaks over the years, but everyone seems much happier about the clarity of the brand."

Neal's Yard's hippie-esque origins remain in place, and quite a few old-school types resisted and resented efforts to make the brand a "God forbid, commercially successful company," as Aboud recalls. "Sure, there was a lot of to-ing and fro-ing within, but thankfully, I don't think we've moved a million miles away from where we started. And the mark is untouched."

We all know how frustrating it can be when what you thought was the jasmine-almond moisturizer turns out to be the witch hazel-based hemorrhoid cream. Sure, the wrinkles go away for a spell, but the embarrassment lasts forever. Design that helps the right ointments go to the right places is good design indeed. Well done, Mr. Aboud.

Neal's Yard Remedies — COVENT GARDEN

Geranium & Orange BATH OIL

Brings a sense of HARMONY

SUNNY ORANGE AND REVITALISING GERANIUM
AROMATHERAPY BLEND FOR LIFTING THE SPIRIT
APRICOT AND WHEATERM OILS NOURISH.

SWIRL THROUGH WARM WATER

MADE IN ENGLAND
THETIC FRAGRANCES OR COLOURS • NO PARABENS • NO

Geranium & Orange SHOWER GEL

To gently cleanse and REVIVE

ESSENTIAL OILS OF GERANIUM & ORANGE IMPART A
BRIGHT, SUNNY SCENT TO LIFT THE SPIRITS, WHILE
ORGANIC EXTRACT OF CALENDULA SOOTHES AND
CONDITIONS THE SKIN

APPLY SPARINGLY FOR A GENTLE CLEANSING ACTION

MAY ALSO BE USED AS A SHAMPOO

MADE IN ENGLAND
TIC FRAGRANCES OR COLOURS • NO PARABENS • NO SILICONES

Seaweed & Arnica FOAMING BATH

A restorative bath to enjoy
when OVERTIRED

S OF MINERAL-RICH SEAWEED, COMFREY AND
RE COMBINED WITH PURE ESSENTIAL OILS
INE, JUNIPER AND LAVENDER TO EASE TIRED
CLES AND RESTORE A SENSE OF VITALITY

UR LIBERALLY UNDER RUNNING TAPS

MADE IN ENGLAND
URS • NO PARABENS • NO SILICONES • NO PHTHAL

Redcat Theater

Animal Magic

"AS DESIGNERS, WE'RE TEMPTED TO MAKE EVERYTHING LOOK WONDERFUL, and most of the time we do, but sometimes it's best to leave a logo alone," Sean Adams says. "But if a mark has little positive equity or negative associations, we look at a redesign or new nomenclature. This can mean a complete overhaul or simple refinement."

AdamsMorioka's Redcat Theater logo is the redesign of a mark that just barely saw the light of day, and yet it's also an object lesson in how building on an identity's equity is always the starting point for designers. Conceived during construction and fund-raising phases of the Roy and Edna Disney CalArts Theater (hence the acronym REDCAT), AdamsMorioka's original logo was only applied to early fund-raising materials, a website, and comps for the building's architect, Frank Gehry.

Roy and Edna Disney|CalArts Theater

Before (top): This early logo for Redcat Theater was developed by AdamsMorioka when the project was still under preparation. As the project neared completion, it needed to be updated.

After (bottom): AdamsMorioka's revamped Redcat logo captures a lively sense of artistic innovation in its bold colors, strong typography, and adoption of the symbol of a leaping cat.

"By the time we got around to designing actual signage a year later, we began to see its limitations," says Adams. "It was already a bit dated and dot-com-y. It screamed 1999. We recognized this was not something you could live with very long." Yet in keeping with Adams' philosophy, there were elements in the original that laid the groundwork for a dynamic new visual personality.

ANIMAL STORIES

In the case of the original Redcat logo, the dated look—not a positive association—meant a thorough revisiting of the mark was necessary. According to Adams, a sudden realization provided the solution. In this case, the elephant in the room was a cat. "We realized we were working overtime at ignoring the

obvious," he says. "If you have a theater named Redcat, people are going to think about—guess what?—a red cat. So we magnified this response," by linking the Redcat name and the image of a dancing cat in the new logo.

It wasn't that the feline theme had never occurred to AdamsMorioka. The original logo had featured custom type that suggested cats' tails. "The concept of using a cat's tail to build the letterforms was a great idea," Adams says, "but in doing so we had made an easily dated logo." For the new visual personality, the custom lettering was developed into a typeface, appropriately titled Cat, used on most of the theater's wayfinding and signage.

The neon trails that bend through Redcat Theater's reflective canopy recall a cat's toy string, an element that was part of AdamsMorioka's original identity concept.

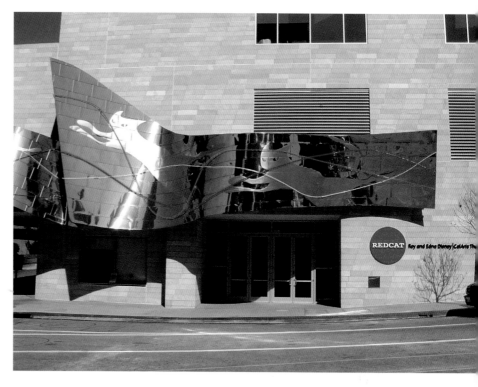

ADDITIONAL EQUITY

The original logo was created in both red and black versions, and this color scheme (with white) was retained in the new solution. Another element was the idea of using a stringlike filament, referencing a cat's toy—a ball of string—in the building's façade. The new logo placed the theater's name in a red circle, this time in bolder serif type, and the string image is now present on the building's canopy, in tracings of brilliant neon.

WHOSE CAT IS THIS ANYWAY?

Along the way, the cat theme was nearly derailed by the challenge of finding the perfect feline. "It turned out that presenting various images of cats was like a Rorschach test," Adams recalls. "Because the theater's governing board and staff all had to be involved in evaluating the design, we discovered that people react to images of cats very differently." One person would think a given image looked angry, another that it was a happy cat.

"Each response was strong—but different," he says. By the time the building neared completion, though, the group had settled on a cat image that was at once joyful, energetic, and emblematic. True to form, this cat image also invites a multitude of interpretations. Is it a pounce or a pirouette?

The final result—a picture of animal ballet, promising classic grace with fresh and fuzzy appeal—is superbly responsive to the Redcat's mission statement, which Adams paraphrases as, "We're your friendly neighborhood avant-garde theater." The solution may look like it was arrived at by alchemy,

some magical way of resolving the wide range of roles and purposes this nationally prominent but fervently local theater fulfills. But AdamsMorioka's Redcat identity is really a matter of discipline, process, observation, understanding context and audience—and respecting equity.

CREATIVE DIRECTORS: SEAN ADAMS, NOREEN MORIOKA
ART DIRECTOR: VOLKER DÜRRE

Hunters & Gatherers

An 'Oxton Swirly Queen!

HUNTERS & GATHERER S WAS ALREADY AN ESTABLISHED DESIGN FORCE IN LONDON'S HIP HOXTON/SHOREDITCH DIS-TRICT. Having started as a stall in the Camden Lock Market, the fashion label had grown in fifteen years to become a brand sold in boutiques worldwide. Building on that success, repositioning the brand for a bold run at the next fifteen years—this was the job that fell to London-based Fridge Creative and the design team of Michael Boston, Anna Hilton, and Nieve Tierney.

Hunters & Gatherers' deepest influences lie in UK pop and street culture, and its determination to offer high fashion at affordable prices is one way the company shows its loyalty to the old neighborhood. But whatever its origins, the actual couture, like Eliza Doolittle, turns out to be pretty posh.

The words that observers use in praise of Hunters & Gatherers' work tend to be luxurious as well. The designs address the "primeval instinct of womankind" and her relationship to the "ritual of dress," according to a leading fashion website (www.fashionmission.nl). A spokesman, explaining the label's name, says: "We chose the name as a reflection of our desire to be inspired from all sources, not just the usual fashion trends. We hunt down beautiful materials, we gather dreams and aspirations."

Above all, these are products meant to stand out, not to blend in. The Hunters & Gatherers motto: "Be a peacock, not a chameleon."

Before (top): The previous identity was clean and efficient. It served the client well, and it defied trends that can age as rapidly as fruit.
After (bottom): The client wanted something that was "bespoke and magical," that was familiar to loyal buyers but somehow renewed. The new look is all that plus the font is the classic Baskerville, an homage to its British heritage.

MESSAGE AND MILIEU
Primeval instincts, rituals of dress, dreams and aspirations, peacocks and chameleons: heady, thrilling stuff—but where fashion is grandiose, identity design must be grounded. Nieve Tierney of Fridge elaborates on her company's approach to rebranding:

"Logos are personal as they mirror our clients services, products, and messages. Often, the client has been using for many years, so approaching the subject of change can be tricky. You need to support your arguments with plenty of research to back up your proposed ideas. Your recommendations need to be based on strategy, not personal likes or dislikes. And because a logo translates our client's voice and message visually to its target audience, we like them to be involved in the design process of a rebrand as much as possible."

HUNTERS AND GATHERERS

Hunters&Gatherers

Hunters&Gatherers

The client felt their affiliation with Shoreditch had a lot of equity. The popular district, which surrounds its residents with stimulation and creativity, is home to design groups of all disciplines and is rich with small pubs and boutiques. For leading designers at Hunters & Gatherers, the Shoreditch milieu wasn't just an influence, but an inspiration—the source of a distinctive character and attitude. Says Tierney, "They wanted the fashion brand to suggest something that was bespoke and magical."

SWIRL POWER

While the client welcomed change, the one aspect of their retiring identity that they did not wish to leave behind was its illustrative elements and qualities. This look lent much personality to the brand and was used in many applications.

"We were keen to use the illustrative style as a branding tool," Tierney recalls. "Producing a set of illustrations for use as a branding palette was a main part of the project. We had a strict brief to reflect the feminine nature of their collection. These elements can be mixed and matched to produce different outcomes, for instance the collections had representative icons taken from our illustrative palette, as well as developed illustrations on the printed materials."

One thing was certain. The logotype had to be replaced. Fridge decided to use Baskerville, a classic English font, as homage to Hunters & Gatherers' British heritage. The ampersand provided a perfect opportunity to add flourish and herald not only the illustrative quality of the other identity elements, but also the flowery accents—"girly and swirly," Tierney calls them—of the clothes themselves.

"In the fashion industry," concludes Tierney, "trends can be fickle. So it is unwise to develop an identity that follows a current trend. They aren't likely to last. Instead, we look to develop a language, a visual personality, that makes buyers and customers feel they are being introduced to a familiar friend. We wanted to produce an iden-

tity that potential clients could relate to. We feel the new identity embodies all of this—it connects with the audience like a new exciting friend. And for newcomers to the brand, it makes a powerful first impression whilst still supporting its feminine origins."

DESIGN DIRECTOR, CREATIVE DIRECTOR, ART DIRECTOR: MICHAEL BOSTON
DESIGNERS, ILLUSTRATORS: NIEVE TIERNEY, ANNA HILTON
COPYWRITER: HUNTERS & GATHERERS

The name Hunters & Gatherers is a subtle reference to primeval instincts of women, ritual of dress, and finding and gathering inspiration from the natural world. And you thought it suggested something naughty, didn't you? Bad girl.

SIECE

Where There's a Quill, There's a Way

DESIGN: CAROL GARCÍA DEL BUSTO
BARCELONA

130

A QUILL PEN IN AN INKPOT, drawn in a gloppy, wobbling line and accented with a scrawl of pastel blue: SIECE's former logo was anything but solemn. For the client, this was precisely the problem.

SIECE stands for the Interdisciplary Seminary for Writing Culture Studies at Alcala University in Madrid: it's a conference for intellectuals, and they didn't want their symbol to be a pen that looked like it was goofing off. The former logo "didn't communicate anything academic," says Carol García del Busto in Barcelona. "It seemed like something from grade school."

García del Busto's redesign gives SIECE a scholarly look. Gone is the purple pastel happy quill and blue pastel ink well. Gone, too, the san serif all-cap, italic font. The new logotype is serif, lowercase and bold, sharper-edged and, because it is partially obscured by the quill, more visually challenging. Seek us out for knowledge. As for that pen—it's now blood red, ready to attack the page. A+.

Before (top left): Influential, grumpy intellectuals thought the previous whimsical illustrated identity was not serious enough for their academic writers conference. Humbug.

After (above): Garcia del Busto of Barcelona gave it a more scholarly, adult look, retaining the quill but making it blood red—and deadly serious.

CREATIVE DIRECTOR, DESIGNER, ILLUSTRATOR:
CAROL GARCÍA DEL BUSTO

California Film Institute
Retrofitted

DESIGN: MINE
SAN FRANCISCO

"THERE'S THIS BEAUTIFUL NEON MARQUEE SIGN THAT LOOKS GREAT LIT UP AT NIGHT," says Chris Simmons, principal of Mine, referring to the Christopher B. Smith Rafael Center.

The Rafael is owned and operated by the California Film Institute (CFI), a nonprofit organization that promotes film as art education through its film screenings and programs at the Rafael, its CFI Education Program, and its internationally known Mill Valley Film Festival.

The beautifully restored Art Deco Rafael theater is a cultural landmark in the heart of downtown San Rafael, and literally where Simmons started when the CFI commissioned him to update and redesign all three of its brands.

Before (left column): The California Film Institute (CFI) is an institution with one famous event, its festival, and a beautiful home, the Rafael Film Center. On its 30th birthday, the directors decided the three entities should look like one happy family.

After (right column): Taking visual cues from the gorgeous art deco Rafael Film Center, Mine united the family without making them look like triplets. Bravo!

"Each year, the institute asks a different designer to do the look and feel for the festival. Mark Foxx designed it one year, and that great Rafael marquee is his, too," says Simmons. Tom Bernaro, Bill Cahan, and many others have donated their services over the years, each creating a unique interpretation.

"When we came on board it was CFI's thirtieth anniversary. 'Turning 30' was their phrase, and they wanted to look at it as more of a birthday and a milestone rather than a look-back type of approach," says Simmons. "So we thought that would be a good opportunity to solidify their identity and make a stronger connection between the institute, which has a vision for film in northern California, the festival, which is what the public interfaces with the most, and the theater, which is the property. They should be a related experience."

Onion Tears. Simmons uses this diagram to demonstrate to clients where design expression lies in the scheme of things. It is the most visible element of the brand but it is not the most important. Design can mask rotten leadership, products, etc., but rot will reveal itself when the onion is peeled.

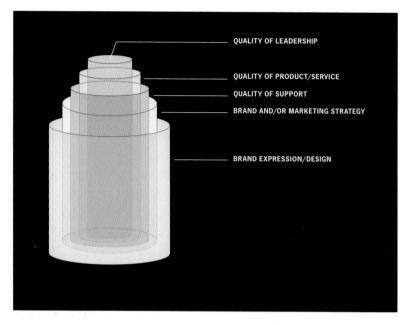

QUALITY OF LEADERSHIP

QUALITY OF PRODUCT/SERVICE

QUALITY OF SUPPORT

BRAND AND/OR MARKETING STRATEGY

BRAND EXPRESSION/DESIGN

Unlike previous years, when designers were asked to design only the festival collateral, Simmons had the opportunity to look at CFI's personality as a whole. "We focused on the festival logo—it's what gets attached to most things. But, we said if we're going to do this we should do it as a package," says Simmons.

The Mill Valley Film Festival is internationally acclaimed for its celebration of the best of independent and world cinema. Highly respected and considered by many to be the launching pad for the Oscar® campaign, the festival is supported and attended by top filmmakers, actors, and film fans.

MARQUEE NAME

"If you took the Mill Valley Festival identity that they had at that point and put it next the other well-known festivals, it wasn't even on par. Not even close. And worse, it didn't even have that kind of niche specificity of an Austin Film Festival or Seattle Film Festival where there are geographic elements that place it in those cities," he says.

Simmons went back to the Rafael marquee neon and built upon it to redefine the personality of all three

logos. "With any redesign, we look to see what already exists, and if there is some existing truth or anchor about who a client is or what they do that we can work from. The Rafael building and its marquee are CFI's greatest and most visible assets, we'd have been foolish to not use it," he says.

Simmons used the Art Deco styling of the Rafael logo and carried it through the logos for the Institute and the CFI Education Program. "We were really trying to focus on creating a visual personality with an updated deco inspired—but not backward-looking—family of identities, a family of colors, consistent type style, and just a basic framework for the overall look and feel."

PEELING AN ONION

The idea of refreshing the brand's visual personality can be a challenge for many clients. To help his clients understand the benefits that can be gained through a redesign, Simmons says he talks not only about what is going to change but what the redesign is *not* going to change. "I have this

MILL VALLEY
FILM FESTIVAL

TURNING 30

Christopher B. Smith
OCTOBER 4-14 | 2007   Rafael Film Center • CineArts @ Sequoia
                           142 Throckmorton Theatre

MILL VALLEY   tickets: 877 874 MVFF mvff.com   Presented by the California Film Institute
FILM FESTIVAL
                                                        Agency: Scheyer/SF Design: MINE™ Printing: Oscar Printing

diagram that I show that's based on something Terry Irwin told me years ago. The diagram is almost like layers of an onion. The center is the leadership, around that is the business plan, and surrounding that you've got your quality or service, then around that is the quality and support of that product,

and then on the outside you have the brand—the visual expression. What I tell them is that, by and large, nothing on the outside is going to affect the inside. Meaning, the outside is not going to make you a great leader, it's not going to make your product better. I think explaining that helps them understand that we respect the value of what they do and we don't overstate our importance."

Simmons offers that this conversation also provides the opportunity to talk about those instances that the outside can affect the inside. "In the instance of CFI, they have a great leadership, a great core of people, and they put on an internationally respected festival. If you wrap all that up in a shoddy identity it can be detrimental because what you're presenting to someone is not living up to who you are," he says.

Simmons says this talk helps to put things in perspective. Expressing that the designer plays a role, and the client plays a role and, that the designer is not the answer to everything but that he/she is there to help people understand whom the client is. "The logo gets its meaning from what it represents, not the other way around," says Simmons.

DESIGN DIRECTOR, CREATIVE DIRECTOR:
CHRISTOPHER SIMMONS
DESIGNERS: CHRISTOPHER SIMMONS,
TIM BELONAX
ORIGINAL RAFAEL THEATER LOGO DESIGN:
MARK FOX

Johnson Favaro

Building Type

MDA JOHNSON FAVARO IS A PRESTIGIOUS TEN-PERSON ARCHITECTURE FIRM IN CULVER CITY, California. It has a nettlesome and unique problem. It was getting lost in the avalanche of proposals that were arriving on its prospects review desks. It desperately needed a new visual approach that would help it stand out. Enter Ph.D.

Steven Johnson, principal of MDA Johnson Favaro said that in follow-up interviews with prospects that had not chosen his firm, he was often told that his proposal's visual presentation did not stand out. Not only was the identity grayish, but the layout of the pages were uninspired, and the images were lifeless.

According to Johnson, "Today it is even harder because whereas before the recession you had to stand out among, say, fifteen firms, today you may see eighty firms competing for the same project." So when the proposal arrives, the cover and the layout must arrest the eye of the reviewers. And, says Johnson, "Previously, our proposals were getting lost in the pile."

So rather than just redesign the proposal format, Johnson Favaro decided to address their entire visual identity system. Wise move. It gave the firm the unique opportunity to reposition themselves and represent themselves to the world.

Before (top): Wallpaper. Who'll pull this off a pile of architecture RFPs?
After (bottom): Outstanding. This one jumps into the prospect's hands.

The first thing the Ph.D team asked the client to do was bring in any reference material it had that it regarded highly. According to Johnson, "They told us it could be anything from anywhere—magazines, books, art, catalogs, packaging. But we ended up bringing in artist and architect monographs—very simple, very graphic, and very beautiful publications with exquisite layout. It gave us the opportunity to express what we wanted out of this assignment."

The next step was for Ph.D to present their initial comps. They showed five, but one immediately stood out above the rest to the team at Johnson. "Right off the bat, we knew this was the right choice," says Johnson. "We liked the bold colors, the use of the white, clean background. We felt it was straightforward and composed, a sensibility that reflects our work. On proposal covers the logotype nearly covers the whole page, really grabbing one's attention. And while the color and boldness are contemporary, the font choice and the composition are flexible and, we hope, enduring."

MDA JOHNSON FAVARO

ARCHITECTURE + URBAN DESIGN

Perhaps some might miss the nuance in the design, but that bothers neither client nor designer. The stacking of the letter *O*'s suggests attention to detail and composition and is also a reference to the partnership of Johnson and coprincipal Jim Favaro. The stacking of the acronym MDA (a legacy name that is required but will fade, like gray, from existence one day soon enough), Johnson and Favaro is intended to suggest the stacking of

Lost In the Crowd
Before (above): Johnson Favaro's plain looking proposals were getting lost in the shuffle.
After (opposite): The new visual personality has the clients talking, and it's all good!

buildings, or the rendering of a façade. In application, the logotype can be used large or small, depending upon the purpose.

"The layout of the logotype, its design, it is like architecture," says Johnson. "It appears constructed. You see stacked things and things that bearing on one another that come together to form an entire wall. A façade. We love that ... joining together letters to create a form. When designing a façade here we look for alignments to add both structural integrity and surprise, just as the *O*'s in this design were used. We have a long name and that trick helps links the two names in interesting ways."

Has it worked? Well, it's getting attention. "In my career, I have rarely seen an architectural firm's identity that motivated me to send a note or make a comment about how bad or good it was. I have rarely heard anyone else make a comment about graphic identity in this business either. But I cannot tell you how many comments we have received. We are getting

remarks from many who've seen the new identity on business cards, letterhead, or at the bottom of an email. I find that remarkable," Johnson says.

But, really, just how bold and colorful is the work of Johnson Favaro?

"Our work does not involve painted colors. We use the color of the materials to enliven space, not bold, painted wall surfaces. In some ways, this identity bends the curve of our firm in a new direction, a good one because our work is classical and composed, like the identity—but the graphic is bold and colorful, something we needed to stand out from the piles of proposal inundating prospective client offices. It is the balance of boldness and restraint that I think accurately represents who we are as a firm," he adds.

Good design informs and delights. Always.

CREATIVE DIRECTOR: MICHAEL HODGSON
DESIGNERS: MICHAEL HODGSON,
DERRICK SCHULTZ, ALICE JOO

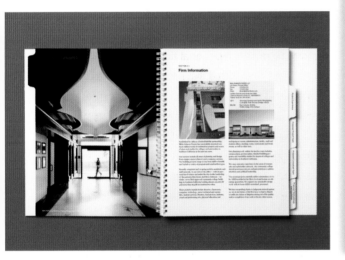

Hawthorne Valley Farm

Sacred Cows

DESIGN: JULIA REICH DESIGN
AURORA, NEW YORK

HAWTHORNE VALLEY FARM, LOCATED IN THE HUDSON VALLEY OF NEW YORK STATE, is a biodynamic agricultural business, and a unique working and educational community. "They adhere to the teachings of an Austrian thinker, Rudolph Steiner—look it up, it's fascinating. The whole place resembles a little German village populated with gentle hippy-types. Brown Swiss cows—affectionately referred to as 'Swissies'—freely roam the surrounding fields," says Julia Reich of Julia Reich Design.

For a long time, the only yogurt product Hawthorne Valley Farm carried was plain yogurt in a quart container. The farm sells the yogurt at their onsite farm store, at New York City's Union Square Greenmarket, and several natural food stores and supermarkets throughout the northeast, so their exposure is limited. But if you think the organic dairy market is peaceful and gentle, think again: competition is fierce, and the explosion in local and organic foods has made it incumbent on enterprises like Hawthorne Valley to present a more professional image on the shelf. Everything from wine to cheese to cereal and pasta sauce now come in the organic variety, so it's critical to build these brands to stand out not only against other organic brands, but amongst the regular—and usually more popular—food brands.

Before (left): Hawthorne Valley Farm's original packaging was as plain as the yogurt inside.
After (bottom right): Julia Reich's identity revamp gives Hawthorne Valley a bright new color palette to go with an expanded product line.

When the farm called Julia Reich, they were expanding their product line, adding a smaller 6-oz. cup and two new flavors as part of a fresh strategy. Hiring a professional graphic designer was

With an untouchable cow, what remained in play were the logo's background, color, and type treatment.

the logical next step. The designer's direct report? The farm manager. The designer's greatest challenge? Flattening a steep learning curve when it came to logos, branding, and graphic design.

Says Reich, "Our charge was to develop cup designs for the two new flavors, while taking into account an expanding color palette that could be used for future yogurt flavors. We were instructed not to touch their logo—that cow was sacred."

COWS ARE NOT FUNNY

The client was comfortable with the cow graphic the way it was: a graceful, serene rendering, meant to show respect for an animal that they felt was too often depicted as cartoonish and silly, like the Borden Corporation's famous mascot, Elsie the Cow, or the lovely and almost timeless La Vache qui Rit, "The Laughing Cow."

With an untouchable cow, what remained in play were the logo's background, color, and type treatment. "We did need to smooth out the line work, which was inconsistently rendered and rough," says Reich. "We also decided to redesign the background landscape, since we decided it was a hard read as mountains and pastures."

The designers also took a wee bit of liberty: they tidied up Serene Sitting Cow's lines to flatter her and make her more legible. "We cleaned her up a little," notes Reich. "We did not change her." Working happily with the farm manager, before he passed it off to his wife, Reich's team got approval for a new label design with refreshed cow and landscape.

Then someone decided to show the new label design to a young woman who had just come to work at the farm. She told the boss that the proximity of the cow's rear to the official USDA Organic seal made the seal look like "poop coming out the cow's butt."

Suddenly the cow was not so sacred. The client instructed Reich to begin exploring new versions of the cow. She began looking for new ways to approach the old cow. "Our office is located in rural central New York, where there are, luckily, lots of dairy farms with cows available to be photographed in various poses," Reich says.

Reich turned the design and the cow around so it faced forward. Eventually, however, the client returned to the previously approved label with the cow facing backwards. The new label was approved and the cups were produced. The new packages hit the shelves in early 2009.

How Now, Brown Cow? After a young farmhand observed that the original version of the logo seemed to make manure out of the USDA Organic seal, Hawthorne Valley Farm's serene cow made a temporary about-face. Though the cow turned back around in the final version, designer Julia Reich still believes we'll get a better look at her one day. "There is no rush," Reich says.

RAIN AND MUD

All of this raises the question: Was the client correct to keep the serene sitting cow exactly as before? Should the designer have been more forceful in advocating for the initial design and, later, for the forward-oriented cow label design? Every case is different. Reich explains:

"Sure, they drove me crazy, but I loved them. The kind people I was dealing with were not visually savvy and did not have experience with graphic design. We talked more about the rain and mud sometimes than anything else. But I look at the bigger picture. The mission of Hawthorne Valley Farm is wonderful. Their products are good for you. I appreciate what they do and I put this at the core of our relationship. I want to help them go to a new level—but things can move organically, slowly. There is no rush."

Every organization has its challenges: design by committee, mean-spiritedness, personal incompetence, and blame passing. Hawthorne Valley Farm might have their own issues, but nothing awful or dispiriting. There was a committee of but two—the farm manager and his wife—and the usual rain and mud were the only "dirty" aspects of the job.

Everything flowed with the natural order. Cows. Sunrise. Sunset. If Reich did not achieve all her goals, she has at least planted the seed. So wait and see: that cow will come around. Julia Reich is patient.

DESIGN DIRECTOR, CREATIVE DIRECTOR, ART DIRECTOR, ILLUSTRATOR: JULIA REICH
DESIGNER: MELISSA CHIOTTI
PRODUCTION ARTIST: MELISSA CHIOTTI

Sony Walkman
It Was 20 Years Ago Today...

DESIGN: SONY CORPORATION
TOKYO

I REMEMBER HAVING DINNER IN NEW YORK IN 1979 WITH A FRIEND OF MINE who was a fashion designer and had just come back from Tokyo. We were with a big group of people, but I was fascinated by the story he was telling me about people listening to music on the subway. "They had personal cassette players, not much bigger than a cassette itself." It seemed totally unreal to me, impossible almost, but it was the birth of The Walkman. Of course, it changed the world in its own way.

Fast forward to 1999 and Sony decided to redesign the Sony Walkman logo to commemorate its 20th anniversary. The brand was in need of a logo that reflected the product's new features—including network compatibility and flash memory—and it needed to be done by Y2K, in time for the launch of the next-generation models.

New technology had completely changed the landscape of portable music devices since Walkman was introduced in 1979. Sony had been there for the entire evolution of recordable media technology—from tapes and discs, to HDD and flash memory. At the time of the rebranding, the technology giant was preparing to re-enter the portable music device market—and with a new logo.

Before (top): Walkman's logo was 20 years old in 1999. For Y2K, Sony decided Walkman needed a new look.

After (bottom): Introduced May 20, 2000, this logo features a *W* that stands for Walkman and a period that is shorthand for the next generation (think Gen X.) The interconnected letters in the logotype symbolize the interconnectivity of modern life.

So how did the process work? First, the visual communication design team sat down with the product design team to prepare a proposal for heads of the brand business unit management team. Once the business unit management team gave the go-ahead to the visual communication design team and the product design team, the real fun began. Initial logo concepts were developed by graphic designers from all global affiliates at that time—Tokyo, Singapore, United Kingdom, and United States—and presented at an internal design competition.

Careful consideration was made to ensure that the mark selected would not date quickly with new designs and iterations of next-generation Walkm[e]n. While the famous name remained, the new logo took nothing from its predecessor. The new logo was introduced 15 May 2000. *W* stands for *Walkman* and the "." symbolizes the next generation. The lines linking the five circles suggest, according to Sony, "connecting individuals together in the network era."

The logo "put[s] more weight on symbolism than on legibility," according to Sony's documents. A Sony spokesperson offered this explanation:

"The shape of the portable audio players has [changed] with the recordable media technology. However, regardless of [these changes], our desire to enjoy music on the go, and the need to use headphones to listen to the music, remains the same…[W]e can use sound, voice and text to communicate 'Walkman' in promotional activities. Upon the logo renewal, we considered that the logo should appeal to one's sense/mind rather than something easy to read…It was quite a challenge to communicate 'Walkman' by the W. symbol only, but we feel it has now been well accepted as the new brand identity."

DESIGNERS: KOUKI YAMAGUCHI, HIROSHIGE FUKUHARA

SEGD
Navigating the Flats

FOR MICHAEL GERICKE, A PARTNER AT PENTAGRAM NY, HIS NEW LOGO AND IDENTITY FOR SEGD (Society of Environmental Graphic Design) was a pro bono project and the client was the board of SEGD. The conversations that took place online after this new design was in place were often critical and sometimes dismissive. That happens frequently when change occurs. You've got to have thick skin in this business.

Gericke recalls that up until being asked to undertake this project he had not had a high regard for SEGD, regarding it more of trade group than a design guild. For him, the new logo is a signal that much about SEGD is changing, for the better, for design.

"I felt SEGD was a trade organization dominated by sign fabricators concerned about the code requirements for the visually impaired—all valid things, but limited. It seemed more interested in making things and the technical requirements, rather than design. I was always a member, but my involvement stopped there. When asked, I told SEGD I would join the board if the organization made a commitment to evolving SEGD into something that was more 3-D-design driven," Gericke said.

Sign Language. A job that started with a redesign of their website quickly evolved into a complete rebranding program. While critics have been vocal, it is clear that SEGD sent a message that design is at core of its mission.
(Before: top, After: bottom)

Under the leadership of Leslie Gallery Dilworth, SEGD made that commitment and Gericke joined the board. Dilworth was determined to evolve SEGD into cooler, hipper, more design aware organization, one that would appeal to a broader audience that could include signage experts, of course, but also people who do interiors, interactive media, dynamic environments, exhibitions, three-dimensional sculptures, and a whole range of other things.

Gericke then explained how he came to do the rebranding program for SEGD: "We did not start with the intent of changing the identity, we started with the task of changing their website—the first window into the organization. The site had cobbled together over time and was user friendly or appealing. It certainly did not convey the spirit of where they wanted to go in the future, nor was it attracting the new audiences."

LET THE FUN BEGIN
Gericke worked with interactive designer Lisa Strausfeld to improve the organization's website and to make it convey a new commitment to 3D design. Naturally, they had to address navigation on the site. That's when the fun began.

"We needed navigation, obviously, so we came up with the idea of creating 3-D menus that could be read as abstract 3-D forms but, at the same

Society for Environmental Graphic Design
**The global community of people working
at the intersection of communication design
and the built environment.**

1000 Vermont Avenue NW, Suite 400
Washington, DC 20005
Tel 202-638-5555 Fax 202-638-0891
www.segd.org

Society for Environmental Graphic Design
**The global community of people working
at the intersection of communication design
and the built environment.**

1000 Vermont Avenue NW, Suite 400
Washington, DC 20005
www.segd.org

Society for Environmental Graphic Design
**The global community of people working
at the intersection of communication design
and the built environment.**

1000 Vermont Avenue NW, Suite 400
Washington, DC 20005
Tel 202-638-5555 Fax 202-638-0891
www.segd.org

SEGD is a non-profit 501(c)3 educational organization

time, could be read in flat applications, too. That menu bar iconography then was made into a new symbol. It replaced a guitar pick-, Eames table-, pork chop–like thingy that lacked meaning," said Gericke.

Meaningless pork chop spat out, what remains is a four-column, four-color logo. Gericke says, "We simplified the menu system into four vertical rectangles that convey a sense of space. They have no fancy drop shadows because we wanted them to read as four elements in dimension or merely as flat graphics. We like that ambiguity. It could be an interactive screen or it could be a graphic on paper."

Bloggers from inside the SEGD membership and outside were unkind when they saw the new logo, in most cases, missing the beauty of its simplicity. They made comments such as, "The rhythm of the overall shape is a little off-putting, disjointed almost;" "I don't read it as three dimensions;" "It doesn't have drop shadows;" "All the type is the same scale;" and "Why is it aligned left?" According to Gericke, this was all deliberate: Pentagram went for simplicity in the color shapes and ambiguity.

They tried hard to not make it stylistic and cleverly avoided easy clichés.

And although it was pro bono, Gericke and his team took it through the same formal process that they would for any other large institutional client. "We thought about the approach, the positioning, how we wanted to change the perceptions of what the SEGD is today: The global community of people working at the intersection of communication design and the built environment," Gericke explains. "It's not about just signage, it's about communicating within a built environment."

Unfortunately, the word *environment* remains. Gericke said that, too, was deliberate. "There was a big discussion about changing the name because it is a bit limiting, because it doesn't include more modern things such as dynamic media displays or exhibitions or interiors or facades. But there was equity in the names, so if we changed it you'd have to invest much time and expense to build up name recognition," he says. And that was not in the cards.

Was there push back on any of this from the board? Not according to Gericke. The board agreed that to only change the site and not the logo would be shortsighted—a waste, really. Gericke convinced them they should look at everything. It was a unanimous—wise choice.

ART DIRECTOR: MICHAEL GERICKE
DESIGNERS: MICHAEL GERICKE, SEONG IM YANG, JENNIFER ROSE
PROJECT MANAGER: GILLIAN DE SOUSA

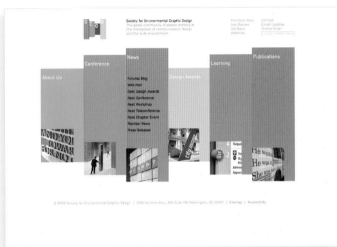

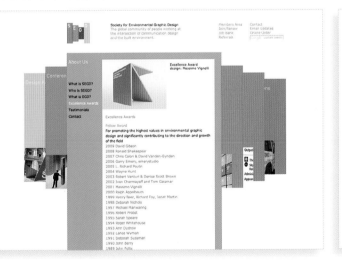

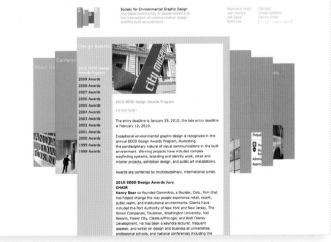

Look Closer. Upon close inspection, the two-dimensional logo created by Pentagram appears three-dimensional. Some environmental (3-D) designers have complained this distinction is too difficult to see in some applications. This begs the question: Just because everyone doesn't get it, does it make a design solution ineffective? Not in our opinion.

Epic Lincolnshire

Green Gothic

DESIGN: ROOT STUDIO
LINCOLN, UNITED KINGDOM

ENGLAND'S ROOT STUDIO REGARDS ITSELF AS "THE MOST ECOFRIENDLY GRAPHIC DESIGN AGENCY IN THE MIDLANDS." It offers clients strategies on how to use recycled materials and eco-friendly processes to reduce their carbon footprint.

When it comes to rebranding, Root is about trimming waste. "We feel that we have an instinct for when a logo has gotten a little bit long in the tooth. Usually you can tell immediately whether a logo appears completely out of date or if it simply needs tidying up a bit," says Tom Bradley, creative director at Root Studio. "But by redesigning or updating the logo we try to make it more efficient and clean-cut by trimming the fat."

Before (top row): The EPIC project and the Lincolnshire's town-supported environmental office were separate but cooperative entities. They then merged.

After (bottom): The new identity kept the silhouette of the town's ancient cathedral, adding it and the town name to the more modern look of the EPIC project's existing identity.

Like most design groups, telling a client their logo is dated and ineffective is delicate work. People invest a lot of themselves in identities, visual personalities, especially smaller enterprises in which founders and owners are still at the pilot's wheel. Thankfully, most new or existing clients realize they have a problem and approach a design professional first. But even ecofriendly Root Studio is not afraid to speak when necessary: "We will mention the possibility of a revamp to clients if we feel that their logo is detracting from their overall product," says Bradley.

Root Studio, EPIC, and LECCAP had been working together for some time before the identity change. Root had created the original LECCAP logo and collateral for EPIC. Since the three shared a business relationship and a passion for ecofriendly solutions,

it was natural that both organizations would ask Root to help create the new, merged identity.

The EPIC stands for Environment, People, Innovation, and Choice. Lincolnshire's main environmental body was LECCAP (Lincolnshire Environmental and Climate Change Action Partnership.) The stated mission of the combined organization is to encourage individuals, businesses, and communities in Lincolnshire to adapt to, or mitigate, the global effects of humanity's activity on the environment. The ultimate goal is a carbon-neutral community. Epic Lincolnshire has a number of important functions: to raise awareness through education, advocacy, and public forums; be an information resource about sustainability; and, finally, help individuals and businesses apply for grants that are available to support their sustainable activities.

From the outset, designers at Root knew both the logos for EPIC and LEC-CAP had equity worth retaining. Says Bradley, "They were relatively straightforward. They were clean and precise. But since neither name had been marked broadly, we felt we could keep the name *EPIC* and drop the acronym *LECCAP*."

Upon receipt of the brief, Root had an in-depth discussion with contacts at the new EPIC Lincolnshire. Says Bradley, "The client immediately agreed there and then that the existing EPIC brand would be the basis for their new logo. However, they also stressed that the local link needed to be reinforced. How the two logos would be merged was left to us."

Good call. Most acronyms are egregious. LECCAP buried the link between Lincolnshire, its symbolic cathedral, and its sustainable mission. Lincoln Cathedral, also known as St. Mary's Cathedral, is the unofficial symbol of Lincolnshire—for good reason. It is one of the finest examples of gothic architecture in England, and it is the town symbol of Lincolnshire. This Anglican cathedral was once believed to have been the tallest building in the world for nearly 250 years. The central spire collapsed in 1549, so no one has even been able to prove the fact, but it is still regarded by some prominent scholars as the most important piece of architecture in the U.K.

Needless to say, Lincoln Cathedral has a lot of equity. It dominated the LECCAP mark. "We kept it in," says Bradley, "and we restored the word *Lincoln* to prominence. We retained the type and coloring from Epic and shape of the LECCAP logo."

In this case, the design team took all the good aspects of the LECCAP identity—the town symbol and the name of the town. They retained all that was fresh, straightforward in the Epic identity—the name (an acronym worth keeping because *Epic* has meaning), the font, and the composition of the type. The colorful waves, suggest joy and vigor.

The end result is an identity that is bold and contemporary, confident and colorful. It is an identity that befits an organization with goals as significant and monumental as Epic Lincolnshire's: a carbon-neutral, sustainable world.

DESIGN DIRECTOR, CREATIVE DIRECTOR:
TOM BRADLEY
ART DIRECTOR: LYDIA SIBSON

Schlegel Bicycles
Recycling the Inlaws

DESIGN: S DESIGN
OKLAHOMA CITY

STEVE SCHLEGEL'S OKLAHOMA CITY BICYCLE BUSINESS WAS A SERIOUS SHOP FOR SERIOUS CYCLISTS—people who knew their Campagnolo from their Shimano, who had chain lube under their nails and scars on their legs, and who'd just rather be riding. Valued as much for their understanding of riders' needs as for their technical knowledge and mechanical skill, Schlegel and his employees were "go-to" sources for equipment and advice for the most dedicated local riders. They had reached out to casual riders and the broader community with public events like "Schlegelfest," an annual safety training day.

Despite a generic name—The Bicycle Store—and a chain-store-ish logo, the business was growing, eventually coming to require both a new location and a serious revisiting of its visual personality. That's when a family connection came into play. S Design founder and principal Sarah Mason Sears is Steve Schlegel's sister-in-law, so when he contemplated the design changes that would reflect his expanded business, he turned to her.

Mucho Merch. Schlegel Bicycles is the name in bikes in Oklahoma City. So what happens when you give it a cool new logo and slap it all over equipment and T-shirts? You sell stuff—lots of stuff—to cool, young, athletic people who look hot in it, who wear it all over town, advertising your name, for free.

MIXED MESSAGES

"Steve had typically traded services and merchandise for marketing and advertising help," says Sears. "The result was about the biggest assortment of what I call 'mixed identity design' I've ever seen. When he told me he was thinking of naming his new location My Bike Store, I said, 'Please don't do that.'"

Sears was familiar with Schlegel's business to know he had a persistent problem with customers confusing his shop with others. The name "My Bike Store," Sears adds dryly, would only make matters worse.

"His business name was so generic, customers had nothing to remember. Once people managed to make it into his shop, they loved the service and the experience. But Steve was losing business before he had a chance to establish a relationship."

When Schlegel hired S Design to investigate a rebrand, he was still set on calling his shop 'My Bike Store.'" Sears says, "I asked him to let us do our groundwork, to be patient. I told him, 'We're going to do it our way *and* your way. And we'll see where we end up.'"

TEAM TRIAL

To focus on what set Schlegel's operation apart from its competitors, Sears and her team asked the proprietor and many of his employees to fill out a detailed questionnaire on what they perceived as the store's attributes.

Enlisting store personnel, Sears says, was critical: "The process often clarifies who they are and what we can do for them—and once we've done the upfront work, everyone 'gets it.' When a client group sees the links between what they told us and the decisions we make, they can get behind our solution."

This investigation, along with research into customer perceptions, revealed that the thing that kept customers coming back to Schlegel was service. "The key attribute we identified was that no matter what kind of rider you are, Schlegel will be able to put you on the kind of bike that's right for you," says Sears. "This gave us the basis to start investigating visual solutions for a new logo."

WHAT TO KEEP, WHAT TO LOSE

The team looked at the identities of regional cycling shops to ensure a new Schlegel logo would stand out, and they explored logos farther afield, including those of motorcycle brands and dealers. Another source of inspiration was the relocated shop's new neighborhood, a gentrifying historic district popularly known as Automobile Alley. "You can see the whole history of transportation in the neighborhood," Sears says. "It's a perfect place for a bicycle shop, and it gave us the idea of visually capitalizing on the historical aspect."

Mindful of the potholes on "retro road," S Design was determined to avoid worn-out tropes. Many of the historically themed visual and typographical styles the team reviewed "just looked too old," according to Sears. "Whatever we were going to do also had to have contemporary relevance, because Schlegel's services and bikes are state of the art."

YOUR SURNAME, SIR

And there was that pesky name issue lurking in the background. The S Design team asked if they could submit some design studies incorporating a new name, Schlegel Bicycles. Although initially reluctant (out of modesty) to brand the business with his own name, Schlegel agreed. "Once Steve saw how the logo captures the personal touch of his family business *and* the distinctive character of his shop and the neighborhood, he knew it was right," Sears recalls, adding slyly: "It might have helped [that] I'm a relative. Maybe it allowed me to push harder."

The best logos are learning experiences for designers and clients alike, which proved true with Schlegel Bicycle's identity. "Clients have their own realities," Sears says. "Designers have to learn to sit still and listen to their clients—and only act once we have all the important information, the raw materials for a design. We call it the difference between baking a cake and decorating one."

Thanks, Sis. Steve Schlegel had it going on. He was the leading bike shop in town. He had great reputation. But, he was too shy to use his good name. He thought that was conceited. Fortunately for Schlegel, his sister-in-law, Sarah Sears, slapped some sense into him and his name on everything: the building, the bags, the gear, the shirts, the staff, etc., etc., etc. Sarah is still waiting for her free water bottle.

ANATOMY OF A CYCLING LOGO

156

CYCLISTS ARE STICKLERS when it comes to getting the details right. Although not much of a rider when the design process started, Sears quickly ramped up on biking history and modern technology. "We picked up a lot of tires and wheels to study," she said. "Proportions, treads, spokes, that kind of thing," she notes. "The pattern had to fit our concept for the logo, but it also had to be representative of the real world and the kind of cyclist Schlegel's shop attracts. If, for example, we got the number or size of the spokes wrong, customers would definitely notice."

Design iterations were progressively refined via feedback from Schlegel and his associates. Once the final mark was approved, an identity document was developed to help the client apply the new mark. Branded merchandise—shirts, mugs, beer glasses (a must for appealing to biking enthusiasts), and more—quickly became common sights on the streets and bike paths of Oklahoma City. "When the merchandise took off, it really convinced the shop of the importance of consistency and continuity throughout the identity system," she says.

GREEN—MOUNTAIN BIKING

ORANGE—GENERAL/BMX

**SILVER/GRAY—ROAD BIKES/TRIATHLON/
HIGH-END CYCLING**

BLUE—FAMILY/KIDS

LIGHT BLUE—WOMEN CYCLISTS

Colors Galore. To refine the system's appeal to the cycling community, S Design also developed a color-themed means of communicating the shop's services and products to customer segments. Although originally designed specifically for the branded merchandise, the color system has been applied in marketing and event graphics.

CREATIVE DIRECTOR: SARAH MASON SEARS
DESIGNER: JESSE JAMES DAVISON
CONTRIBUTING DESIGNERS: CARA SANDERS ROBB, JERILYN ARTHUR
ADDITIONAL PROJECTS: TIM BROWN, KYLE REIMER

Tubes and Tires. Know the difference between a tube and a tire? Know how many spokes on a wheel? Sprockets on a gear? Links in a chain? Bike enthusiasts do. And any new logo design that failed on the details risked getting laughed out of Oklahoma City. S Design created a wide variety of design options for the client to choose from—all of them correct.
(Before: left, After: below)

Noggy
Chocolate Change

DESIGN: LATIN BRAND
QUITO, ECUADOR

"IN COLOMBIA, MANY GROCERIES AND SMALL SHOPS HAVE A PECULIAR CUSTOM: They use Noggy as change when the shopkeeper doesn't have spare pennies, and everyone happily accepts," says Silvio Giorgi of Latinbrand.

Ferrero, the global chocolate and confections maker that produces Rocher, Tic Tac, and Nutella—everything from gourmet bonbons to the famous rattling breath mints—knows how to match a product to a market. "That is why they produce Noggy chocolate here. It is a very well-known brand in Latin America," says Giorgi.

In December 2007, Noggy approached Latinbrand in Quito, Ecuador, for assistance. Latinbrand did their homework: research showed that the brand's messages were not connecting with their intended audiences. Older folks loved the brand, but younger audiences were turning to other local brands.

Penny Candy. Noggy chocolate was popular enough in Colombia to serve as small change, but its former logo was one that only an abuelita could love.
(Before: below, After: opposite page)

GRANNY WRAPPER

"At first, our focus was only the packaging. It was old fashioned and dated. But it became clear that the logotype was such an integral and dominant part of the package that it needed to be addressed, too," says Giorgi.

"In Ecuador, chocolate is a popular gift for any love situation," adds Giorgi. "But it seemed that only grandmothers were buying the Noggy gift boxes because they loved the old-fashioned packaging that made it look like a present. So when we say 'old fashioned,' we are not kidding."

Latinbrand kept the name but added more colors, giving the package a kind of M&M look. (Like M&M, Noggy chocolates are contained in a candy shell, a practical consideration in tropical climates such as Ecuador and Colombia.) The logotype was redesigned with a friendlier, more modern typeface. It also made the word *Noggy* primary, and reduced the size of *Ferrero* on the new packaging.

"We took a risk, but Ferrero liked it," Giorgi reports with relish. "The packaging is cleaner and more conceptual. Noggy packs a big taste in a small candy, so even the enlarged logotype on the package is making a subtle point about freshness and taste."

Small candy. Big taste. Nice work. Sweet.

DESIGN DIRECTOR: SANDRO GIORGI
CREATIVE DIRECTOR, ART DIRECTOR:
SILVIO GIORGI

The International Symbol of Access

Murphy's Start

BRENDÁN MURPHY,
UNIVERSITY OF CINCINNATI

BRENDÁN MURPHY NOW SENIOR PARTNER AT LIPPINCOTT, NEW YORK, designed this symbol in 1994 while a graduate student at the University of Cincinnati. He had been looking for a thesis subject and had come across an article by Paul Arthur calling for the redesign of the handicap symbol. Arthur (1924–2001) was a British-born Canadian graphic designer who invented pictographs as we know them and claimed credit for coining the terms *signage* and *wayfinding*. He was the author of several books, including *Wayfinding: People, Signs, and Architecture*.

Murphy continues the story: "When I looked into the meaning of the word *handicapped* (literally meaning cap in hand) I found it very disturbing. My dad grew up in Dublin around the corner from Christy Brown, and his story, *My Left Foot*, had always inspired me. He fought to be seen for his artistic and intellectual abilities, and not to be defined by his physical disabilities. I saw this as an opportunity for design to redefine how people look at each other and at the world."

Brendán Murphy discovered that handicap meant "hat in hand," a discovery he found disturbing when conducting research for ths project. So he gave the symbol new meaning as a person in a vehicle that suggests progress, action, and independence. Did it make a difference? Murphy's symbol has been adopted by organizations, cities, and businesses all over the world.
(Before: below, After: opposite page)

In designing this symbol, Murphy tried to be sensitive to both the message and the audience. Both in word and image he sought to move away from the label "handicapped." With the new symbol for accessibility, the chair no longer imprisons the person—the chair is merely the vehicle with which he or she gains access. Activity and movement are suggested with body positioning—the angle of the torso and the "pushing position" of the arm. The goal was to portray an active, independent person, in sharp contrast to the former symbol that has been described as dependent, rigid, and helpless.

Despite the sometimes conservative nature of signage design, Murphy's new symbol is already in use throughout the world, thanks in large part to the ranks of SEGD. Chris Calori included it in her new textbook on wayfinding. Someone recently sent Brendán a photo of it in use in Korea; it is used in the new MoMA, New York, the new sign program at Walmart uses it. The City of San Antonio adopted it soon after its design, as did Rei. And of course, Ph.D uses it on every job they can.

Cheers, Brendán—stout work!

DESIGNER: BRENDÁN MURPHY

BEST PRACTICES
TEAM U.S. POSTAL SERVICE
Dude, This is Tight!

AUTHOR'S NOTE: AS A DESIGNER AND AN AVID CYCLIST, I've always been curious about the jersey the Lance Armstrong–led
US Postal Service team wore on the last day of the Tour de France in 2003. So I'm very excited to have tracked down the
designer James Selman and to tell the story in this book.

Knowing victory was close in hand, Armstrong and his USPS teammates rode the final stage wearing an entirely new
team kit: gray uniforms featuring the old USPS "U.S. Mail" logo. Previously, Armstrong and team had been wearing their
sponsor's official logo and colors. It was the first time any team had ever changed colors on the final day of this great event.

James Selman of weights&pulleys in Portland, Oregon, was working for Wieden + Kennedy's Nike group at the time. He
was the resident cyclist at W+K during his tenure and in 2002, he had the idea of doing this retro jersey—he was a fan of the
old "U.S. Mail" mark, which he saw every day on his street. A year later, he redesigned the existing kit using this old logo and
emailed it to Armstrong in late May, two months before the Tour de France. According to Mr. Selman, "Lance loved it and
immediately sent it to his U.S. Postal Service contact. Nike jumped on the idea, cranked it out, and had it ready in time for
the tour in July. It was a great feat by all parties to pull off in that short time."

Selman was in Paris to witness
this historic fifth victory. He recalls
the moment:

"[Teammate] George Hincapie
(and the rest of the team) were super-
excited by having something special
riding into Paris. George looked at
me and said, 'This is tight.' And I think
Lance was happy because he's such
a huge team guy. So having the yellow stars in the U.S. Mail logo allowed
every member of the team to share
a little bit of yellow on the Champs
Élysées that day—a nice coincidental

Sacre Gris! United States Postal Service riders Lance Armstrong and Viatcheslav Ekimov smiled on the road
to Paris in 2003. Thanks to James Selman's retro jersey, victory wasn't just sweet—it was tight.
(Before: left, After: right)

detail that happened when he received the official logo: nine yellow stars in the old logo and there being nine riders on a Grand Tour team. The support of the team was great. It remains one of the favorite kits of that era."

Even the client was happy with the retro look, according to Selman: "This kit was only used that final day in 2003 and once more a month later at the San Francisco Grand Prix. Lance was stoked on it, so the Postal Service and Nike were happy producing it. I assume

they saw its value, the history, the conversations it started, etc. And the Americans in the crowd that day loved it. I'm not really sure what the French public thought."

Armstrong did not actually wear the retro kit to the podium, he changed back to the official blue strip before taking the stand. His team was actually fined during sign-in for the kit change but they didn't seem to mind for they went on to produce special kits the next two years for the ride into Paris, another with the USPS and one with Discovery Channel.

The vintage USPS logo on the gray kit featured an eagle surrounded by yellow stars, enabling the whole team to share in the color of cycling glory. (Before: above, After: opposite)

DESIGNER: JAMES SELMAN
DESIGN (ORIGINAL BLUE KIT): NIKE, INC.
PRODUCTION: NIKE, INC
PHOTOGRAPHER: PAGE 162. GRAHAM WATSON

SECTION 3: Logo Gallery

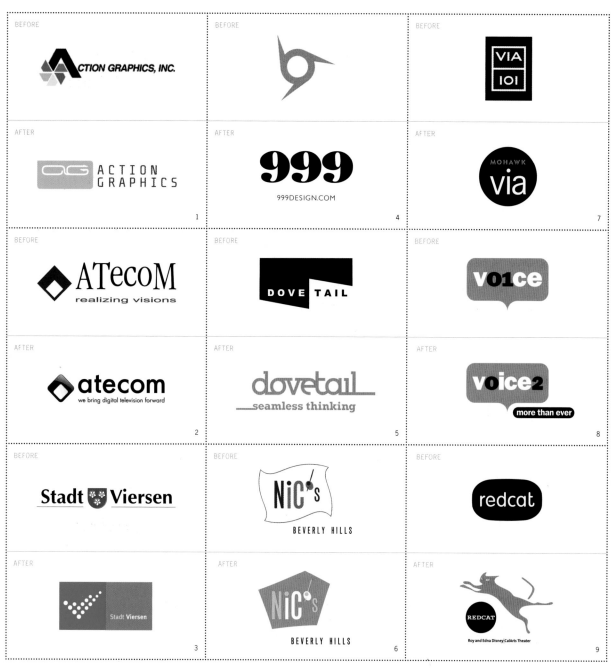

3RD EDGE COMMUNICATIONS
1. Action Graphics
28 LIMITED BRAND
2. Atecom
3. Stadt Viersen

999 DESIGN
4. 999 Design
5. Dove Tail
ADAMSMORIOKA, INC.
6. Nic's Beverly Hills

7. Mohawk Via
8. AIGA Voice
9. Redcat Theater

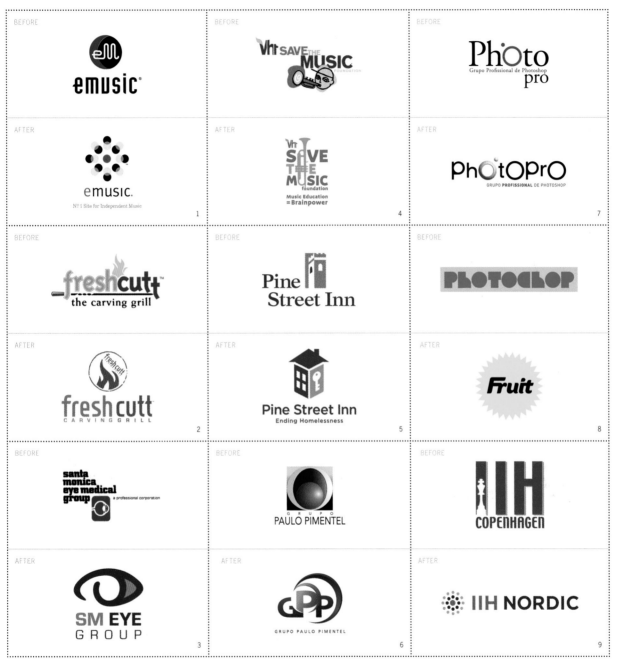

BEFORE

AFTER

Nº1 Site for Independent Music

1

BEFORE

AFTER

CARVING GRILL

2

BEFORE

AFTER

SM EYE
GROUP

3

BEFORE

AFTER

Music Education
= Brainpower

4

BEFORE

Pine
Street Inn

AFTER

Pine Street Inn
Ending Homelessness

5

BEFORE

GRUPO
PAULO PIMENTEL

AFTER

GRUPO PAULO PIMENTEL

6

BEFORE

AFTER

GRUPO PROFISSIONAL DE PHOTOSHOP

7

BEFORE

AFTER

Fruit

8

BEFORE

AFTER

IIH NORDIC

9

ADRIANE DE LOIA
1. E Music
AKAR STUDIOS
2. Fresh Cutt
3. SM Eye Group

ALEXANDER ISLEY INC.
4. VHI Save the Music
BRADHAM DESIGN
5. Pine Streen Inn
BRAINBOX DESIGN ESTRATÉGICO
6. GPP

7. Photo Pro
BRANDCENTRAL:
8. Fruit Imaging
9. IIH Nordic

BRONSON MA CREATIVE
1. Parago
COLLINS:
2. Kodak
CARBONE SMOLAN
3. Bideawee

4. Brooklyn Botanic Garden
5. Hartford Stage
6. The Jewish Museum

CARMIT DESIGN
7. Continuum Capital
CAROL GARCIA DEL BUSTO
8. Siece
CHEN DESIGN ASSOCIATES
9. Public Policy Institue of California

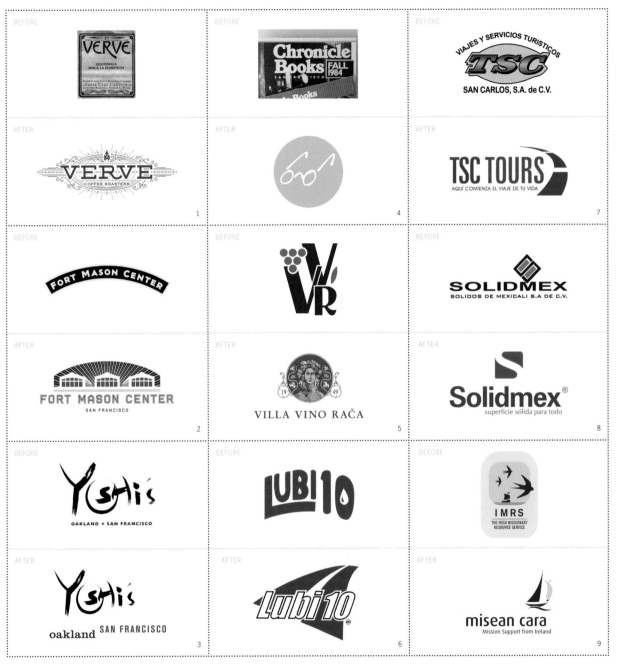

CHEN DESIGN ASSOCIATES
1. Verve
2. Fort Mason Center
3. Yoshi's

CHRONICLE BOOKS
4. Chronicle Books
COMMUNICATION AGENCY
5. Villa Vino Raca
DANIEL TORRES
6. Lubi 10

7. TSC Tours
8. Solidmex
DOUBLE O DESIGN
9. Misean Cara

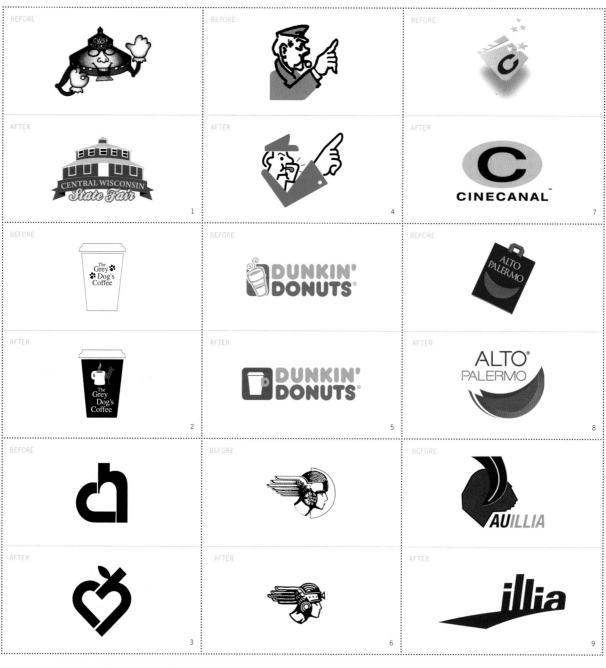

BEFORE

AFTER

CENTRAL WISCONSIN
State Fair

1

BEFORE

AFTER

The Grey Dog's Coffee

2

BEFORE

AFTER

3

BEFORE

AFTER

4

BEFORE

DUNKIN' DONUTS®

AFTER

DUNKIN' DONUTS®

5

BEFORE

AFTER

6

BEFORE

AFTER

CINECANAL™

C

7

BEFORE

ALTO PALERMO

AFTER

ALTO® PALERMO

8

BEFORE

AUILLIA

AFTER

illia

9

ERIK BORRESON DESIGN
1. Central Wisconsin State Fair
FELIX SOCKWELL, LLC
2. Grey Dog's Coffee
3. City Harvest

4. Monopoly
5. Dunkin' Donuts
6. Angelika

FILENI FILNEI DESIGN
7. Cinecanal
8. Alto Palermo
9. Illia

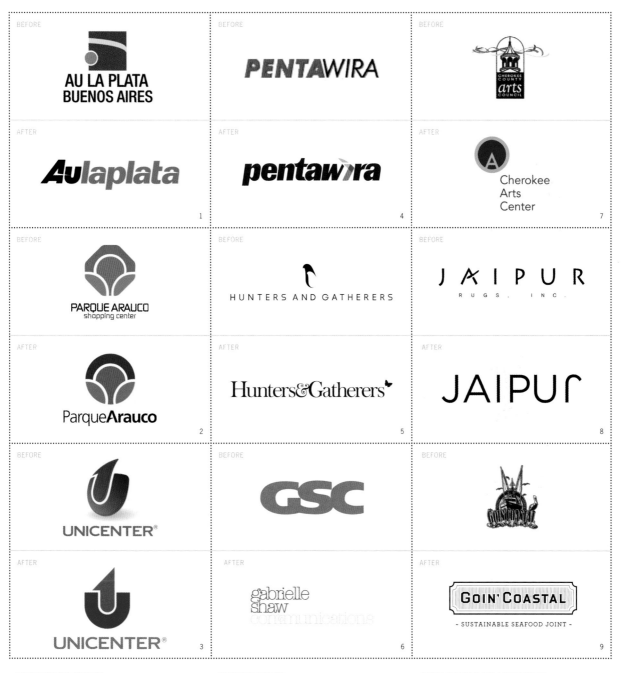

FILENI FILENI DESIGN
1. Au La Plata
2. Parque Arauco
3. Unicenter

FRESH CREATIVE
4. Pentawira
FRIDGE CREATIVE
5. Hunters & Gatherers
6. Gabrielle Shaw Communications

GRANT DESIGN COLLABORATIVE
7. Cherokee Arts Center
8. Jaipur
9. Goin' Coastal

GRAMMA
1. Gramma
GRAVITY INC.
2. CCAB
3. CPO

GRECO DESIGN
4. Criativa
HAMAGAMI/CARROLL, INC.
5. Grand Meadows
6. Aroma Coffee

7. DDD
8. Altrio
9. Hamagami/Carroll, Inc.

BEFORE

AFTER

SO
• wear it declare it •

S❀

1

BEFORE

AFTER

Specialty's
Cafe & Bakery

SPECIALTY'S
Cafe & Bakery
MADE FROM SCRATCH

2

BEFORE

AFTER

Bio Win

BioWin

3

BEFORE

AFTER

SESAR

SESAR
JOINT UNDERTAKING

4

BEFORE

AFTER

CPVO
Community Plant Variety Office

5

BEFORE

AFTER

UBA

UBA

6

BEFORE

AFTER

INNOVATIVE
interfaces

Innovative
interfaces

7

BEFORE

AFTER

HAWTHORNE VALLEY FARM
MADE ON OUR FARM

Hawthorne Valley Farm
USDA ORGANIC
MAPLE VANILLA
Biodynamic®
Organic Yogurt

8

BEFORE

AFTER

Fitucci Windows & doors Co.

FITUCCI
CUSTOM WINDOWS & DOORS

9

HATCH DESIGN
1. SO
2. Specialty's
HOET HOET:
3. Bio Win

4. Sesar
5. CPVO
6. UBA

INNOVATIVE INTERFACES
7. Innovative Interfaces
JULIA REICH DESIGN
8. Hawthorne Valley Yogurt
JUST CREATIVE DESIGN
9. Fitucci

BEFORE

AFTER

METWEST

1

BEFORE

AFTER

Prostate Cancer Foundation

2

BEFORE

AFTER

BCI {GROUP}

3

BEFORE

Sparr Building and Farm Supply

AFTER

SPARR.

4

BEFORE

THE PERSONAL FINANCIAL ADVISORS OF AMERICAN EXPRESS

AFTER

Ameriprise Financial

5

BEFORE

The BANK of NEW YORK

AFTER

THE BANK OF NEW YORK MELLON

6

BEFORE

Delta

AFTER

DELTA

7

BEFORE

Intuit

AFTER

Intuit.

8

BEFORE

Meredith CORPORATION

AFTER

meredith

9

KBDA
1. MetWest
2. Prostate Cancer Foundation
KINESIS
3. BCI Group

KIP CREATIVE
4. SPARR
LIPPINCOTT
5. Ameriprise
6. The Bank of New York Mellon

7. Delta
8. Intuit
9. Meredith

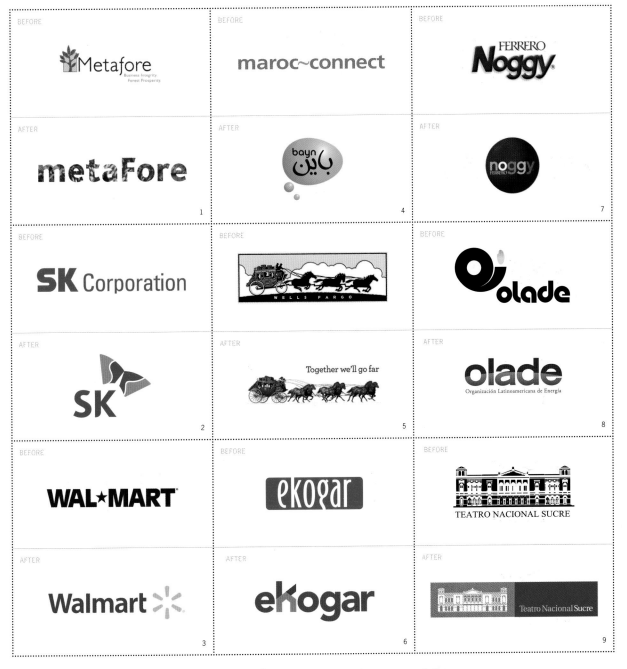

LIPPINCOTT

1. Metafore
2. SK Corporation
3. Walmart

4. Wayne Bayne
5. Wells Fargo

LATINBRAND

6. Ekogar

7. Noggy
8. Olade
9. Teatro Nacional Sucre

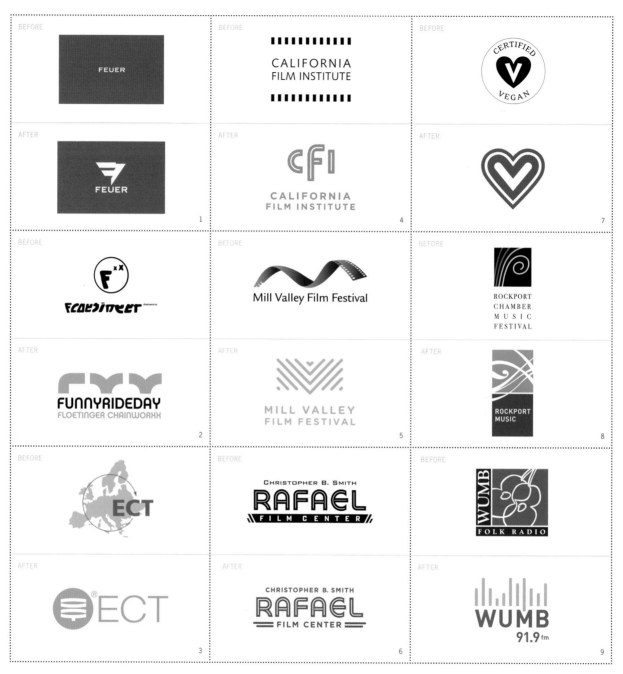

MAURICEREDMOND.COM
1. Feuer
2. FXX
3. ECT

MINE
4. California Film Institute
5. Mill Valley Film Festival
6. Rafael Film Festival

7. Certified Vegan
MINELLI INC.
8. Rockport Music
9. WUMB

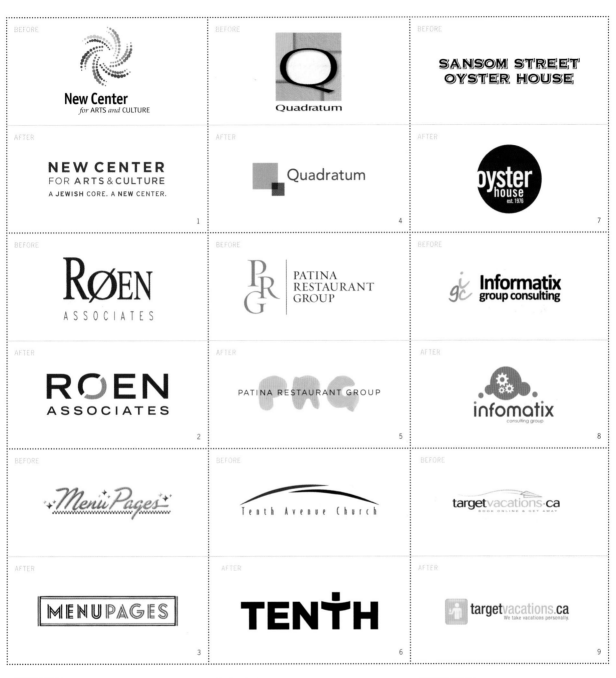

MINELLI INC.
1. New Center for Arts & Culture
MARY HUTCHINSON DESIGN
2. Roen Associates
MUCCA DESIGN
3. Menu Pages

4. Quadratum
5. Patina Restaurant Group
NANCY WU DESIGN
6. Tenth Avenue Church

ORGANIC GRID
7. Sansom Street Oyster House
ONE METHOD INC. DIGITAL & DESIGN
8. Informatix
9. targetvacations.Ca

BEFORE

Travel America Inc.

AFTER

travelamerica

1

BEFORE

La Baguette®

AFTER

LaBaguette
Since 1983

2

BEFORE

KGL
LOGISTICS

AFTER

KGL
LOGISTICS

3

BEFORE

KGL
PORTS INTERNATIONAL

AFTER

KGL
الدولية للموانيء
Ports International

4

BEFORE

KGL
STEVEDORING

AFTER

· We · KGL · STEVEDORING · union ·
Lift Beyond Expectation

5

BEFORE

KGL
TRANSPORTATION

AFTER

KGL
Transportation Company K.S.C.

6

BEFORE

GULF CRAFTS Co. W.L.L.
شركة الخليج كرافتس
Signs & Awards

AFTER

gulfcrafts
شركة الخليج كرافتس

7

BEFORE

SAKS
FIFTH
AVENUE

AFTER

Saks
Fifth
Avenue

8

BEFORE

apnd

AFTER

apnd
ASSOCIATION OF PERINATAL
NATUROPATHIC DOCTORS

9

PAGE 84 DESIGN
1. Travel America
PARAGON MARKETING COMMUNICATIONS
2. LaBaguette
3. KGL Logistics

4. KGL Ports International
5. KGL Stevedoring
6. KGL Transportation

PENGUIN CUBE
7. Gulfcrafts
PENTAGRAM DESIGN
8. Saks Fifth Avenue
PLANK CREATIVE
9. APND

BEFORE

RPMC

AFTER

RPMC

1

BEFORE

INNER-CITY KIDS
INNER-CITY ARTS

AFTER

INNER-CITYARTS

4

BEFORE

TEAM 7

AFTER

TEAM 7®

7

BEFORE

Gunlocke ®

AFTER

Gunlocke®

2

BEFORE

world*aids*
campaign

AFTER

WORLD
AIDS
CAMPAIGN

5

BEFORE

Los Angeles Times Magazine

AFTER

LA

8

BEFORE

MDA JOHNSON FAVARO
Architecture | Urban Design

AFTER

MDA
JOHNSON
FAVARO

3

BEFORE

developmentor

AFTER

DEVELOPMENTOR

6

BEFORE

UNISOURCE SOLUTIONS

AFTER

UNISOURCE SOLUTIONS

9

PH.D, A DESIGN STUDIO
1. RPMC
2. Gunlocke
3. MDA Johnson Favaro

4. Inner City Arts
5. World AIDS Campaign
6. Developmentor

PROPELLA, KONZEPT + DESIGN
7. Team 7
RIP GEORGES + ASSOCIATES
8. LA Times
ROBERT BYNDER DESIGN, INC.
9. Unisource Solutions

R & MAG GRAPHIC DESIGN

1. Casolaro
2. Crispo
3. Hotel Gardenia

4. La Sorgente
5. Nardelli
6. Hotel Plaza

7. Riviera Grand Hotel
8. Hotel Tirrenia
9. Mennella

RAINERI DESIGN
1. Agnellini
2. Distillerie Franciacorta
3. Punto Shop

ROOT STUDIO
4. Epic Lincolnshire
ROSKELLY INC.
5. Red Jacket Resorts
S DESIGN, INC.
6. Schlegel Bicycles

SBOTHRA.COM
7. Rajasthali
SEBASTIANY BRANDING DESIGN
8. Cebrace
9. Ecolabor

BEFORE

LOURIE & CUTLER . P.C.
ATTORNEYS AT LAW

AFTER

LOURIE & CUTLER
Tax, Estate and Business Counsel

1

BEFORE

≡ econveyance
by remoteLaw

AFTER

econveyance™

2

BEFORE

ClearPath

AFTER

clearpath

3

BEFORE

WALKMAN

AFTER

WALKMAN
WALKMAN

4

BEFORE

City of Kelowna

AFTER

City of
Kelowna

5

BEFORE

BALLET KELOWNA

AFTER

Ballet
Kelowna
David LaHay Artistic Director

6

BEFORE

>>
FFun
Motor Group

AFTER

FFUN >> motor group

7

BEFORE

1410
the buzz ⟶⟋⟍⟶ of vancouver

AFTER

TALK 1410AM
The Buzz of Vancouver

8

BEFORE

AFTER

9

SELTZER DESIGN
1. Lourie & Cutler
SMASH LAB
2. Econveyance
3. Clearpath

SONY CORPORATION
4. Walkman
SPLASH DESIGN
5. City of Kelowna
6. Ballet Kelowna

SPRING
7. FFun Motor Group
8. Talk 1410AM
9. The Shrunks

SPRING

1. Moraine Lake Lodge
2. Living Room Pharmacy

STERLING BRANDS

3. Optimum Online

4. Burger King
5. Celestial Seasonings
6. Hellmann's

SUBSTANCE 151

7. HR Anew

STUDIO BLUE

8. CJE Senior Life
9. Chapin Hall

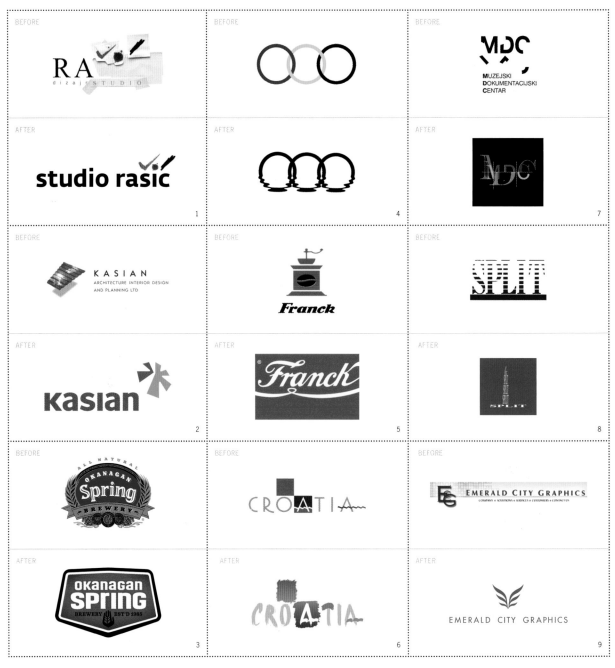

STUDIO RASIC

1. Studio Rasic

SUBPLOT DESIGN INC.

2. Kasian

3. Okanagan Spring

STUDIO INTERNATIONAL

4. Mediterranean Games

5. Franck

6. Croatia

7. MDC

8. Split

tmarks

9. Emerald City Graphics

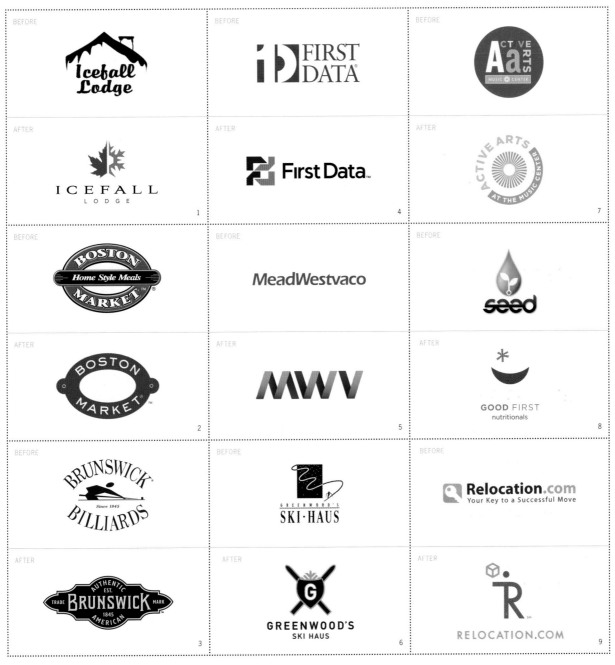

BEFORE

AFTER

Icefall Lodge

ICEFALL
LODGE

1

BEFORE

BOSTON
Home Style Meals
MARKET™

AFTER

BOSTON
MARKET®

2

BEFORE

BRUNSWICK®
BILLIARDS
Since 1845

AFTER

AUTHENTIC
EST.
TRADE BRUNSWICK MARK
1845
AMERICAN

3

BEFORE

iD FIRST
DATA

AFTER

First Data™

4

BEFORE

MeadWestvaco

AFTER

MWV

5

BEFORE

GREENWOOD'S
SKI·HAUS

AFTER

GREENWOOD'S
SKI HAUS

6

BEFORE

ACTIVE
Aa RTS
MUSIC CENTER

AFTER

ACTIVE ARTS
AT THE MUSIC CENTER

7

BEFORE

seed

AFTER

*

GOOD FIRST
nutritionals

8

BEFORE

Relocation.com
Your Key to a Successful Move

AFTER

R℠
RELOCATION.COM

9

THREE 76 DESIGN
1. Icefall Lodge
VSA:
2. Boston Market
3. Brunswick

4. First Data
5. MWV
W DESIGN
6. Greenwood's Ski Haus

WONGDOODY
7. Active Arts at the Music Center
8. Good First
9. Relocation.com

DIRECTORY OF CONTRIBUTORS

3rd Edge Communications
Robert S. Monroe
162 Newark Ave., 3rd Floor
Jersey City, NJ 07302
USA
201 395 9960
www.3rdedge.com
Page 168

28 Limited Brand
Mirco Kurth
Bessemerstr 85, Halle 8
44793 Bochum
Germany
0234 916095-1
www.twenty-eight.de
Pages 64–67, 168

999 Design
Rob Seeney
91–93 Great Eastern St.
London EC2A 3HZ
England
44 0 207 613 1144
www.999design.com
Page 168

Aboud Creative
Alan Aboud
Studio 26 Pall Mall Deposit
124–128 Barlby Road
London W10 6BL
England
44 20 8968 6143
www.aboud-creative.com
Pages 68–73, 120–123

AdamsMorioka, Inc.
Sean Adams
8484 Wilshire Blvd., Suite 600
Beverly Hills, CA 90211
USA
323 966 5990
www.adamsmorioka.com
Pages 86–89, 124–125, 168

Adrianne De Loia
76 Saint Marks Place, 2C
New York, NY 10003
USA
917 806 3312
www.adriannedeloia.com
Page 169

Akar Studios
1404 Third Street Promenade
Suite 201
Santa Monica, CA 90401
USA
310 393 0625
www.akarstudios.com
Page 169

Alexander Isley Inc.
Alex Isley
9 Brookside Place
Redding, CT 06896
USA
203 544 9692
www.alexanderisley.com
Page 169

Bradham Design
Nancy Ide Bradham
683 Great Plain Ave.
Needham, MA 02492
USA
781 444 3554
www.bradhamdesign.com
Page 169

Brainbox Design Estratégico
José Henrique Havro Rodrigues
Praca Osorio 45 Sala 502 Centro
Curitiba PR, 80020.930
Brazil
41 3018 1695
www.brainboxdesign.com.br
Page 169

Brandcentral
Gerard Whelan
6 Clare Street, Dublin 2
Ireland
353 87 322 9901
www.brandcentral.ie
Page 169

Bronson Ma Creative
Bronson Ma
17706 Copper Sunset
San Antonio, TX 78232
USA
214 457 5615
www.bronsonma.com
Page 170

Carbone Smolan Agency
Ken Carbone
22 West 19th Street, 10th Floor
New York, NY 10011
USA
212 807 0011
www.carbonesmolan.com
Pages 100–101, 114–115, 170

Carmit Design
Carmit Haller
2208 Bettina Ave.
Belmont, CA 94002
USA
650 654 3944
www.carmitdesign.com
Page 170

Carol García del Busto
Consejo de Ciento 432, 2-7
08013 Barcelona
Spain
34 609 62 30 55
Pages 130–131, 170

Chen Design Associates
Joshua C. Chen
632 Commercial Street, 5th Floor
San Francisco, CA 94111
USA
415 896 5338
www.chendesign.com
Pages 116–119, 170–171

Chronicle Books
Michael Carabetta
680 Second St.
San Francisco, CA 94107
USA
415 537 4200
www.chroniclebooks.com
Pages 82–85, 171

Collins:
Brian Collins
71 Fifth Avenue, 4th Floor
New York, NY 10003
USA
212 763 4687
www.collins1.com
Page 170

Communication Agency
Pavel Surovy
Jungmannova 4, 85 101
Bratislava
Slovakia
+421 907 915 937
www.communicationagency.com
Page 171

Daniel Torres
Ma Rodriguiz del Toro 1590
Col. Insurgentes Este.
Mexlicali, Baja California,
Mexico
564 00 33
www.danieltorresdg.com
Page 171

Double O Design
Niall Wilson
Rockhill Main Street
Blackrock Co. Dublin
Ireland
353 0 1 764 2001
www.doubleodesign.ie
Page 171

Erik Borreson Design
Erik Borreson
619 Laurel Court, #201
Marshfield, WI 54449
USA
Page 172

Felix Sockwell, LLC
Felix Sockwell
22 Girard Place
Maplewood, NJ 07040
USA
917 657 8880
www.felixsockwell.com
Pages 172, 173

Fileni Fileni Design
Martin Fileni
Av. Alem 592, Piso 14, Catalinas
C1001AAN Buenos Aires
Argentina
54 11 43 13 22 62
www.filenifileni.com
Page 172

Fresh Creative
Imelda Dewajani
Graha Irama Building, Unit 6F
Jl. HR Rasuna Said Blok X1 Kav. 1-2
Jakarta 12950
Indonesia
62 21 521 0851
www.freshandcreative.com
Page 173

Fridge Creative
Nieve Tierney
59 Charlotte Rd.
Hoxton, London EC2 A3QT
England
020 7729 8661
www.fridgecreative.co.uk
Pages 126–129, 173

Gramma
Barbara Bottazzini
Via E. Fonesca Pimentel
7 20127 Milan
Italy
39 02 28970619
www.grammacomunicazione.it
Page 174

Grant Design Collaborative Kurt
Seidel/Bill Grant
11 East Marietta St.
Canton, GA 30114
USA
770 479 8280
www.grantcollaborative.com
Pages 102–105, 173

Gravity Inc.
Wendy Gray
4 Fenwick Ave.
Toronto, ON M4K 3H3
Canada
416 406 3482
www.gravityinc.ca
Page 174

Greco Design
Gustavo Greco Lisita
Rua Rio Verde, 150 Sion—CEP
Belo Horizonte—MG 30310-750
Brazil
55 31 3287 5835
www.grecodesign.com.br
Page 174

Hamagami/Carroll, Inc.
Justin Carroll
John Hamagami
2256 Barry Ave.
Los Angeles, CA 90064
USA
310 458 7600
www.hcassociates.com
Page 174

Hatch Design
Katie Jain
353 Broadway Street
San Francisco, CA 94133
USA
415 398 1650
www.hatchsf.com
Page 175

Hoet Hoet
Nick Hoet
Chaussee De Lasne, 43
1330 Rixensart
Belgium
32 2 646 40 06
www.hoet-hoet.eu
Page 175

Innovative Interfaces
Dean Hunsaker
5850 Shellmound Way
Emeryville, CA 94608
USA
510 655 6200
www.iii.com
Page 175

Julia Reich Designs
Julia Reich
3377 Cork Street
Scipio Center, NY 13147
USA
315 364 7190
www.juliareichdesign.com
Pages 140–143, 175

Just Creative Design
Jacob Cass
PO Box 170
Cardiff 2285
Australia
0411402312
www.justcreativedesign.com
Page 175

KBDA
Kim Baer
2452 Wilshire Blvd., Suite 1
Santa Monica, CA 90403
USA
310 255 0902
www.kbda.com
Page 176

Kinesis
Shawn Busse
30 NW 10th Ave.
Portland, OR 97209
USA
503 922 2289
www.kinesisinc.com
Page 176

Kip Creative
Kip G. Williams
3405 NE 33rd Ave.
Ocala, FL 34479
USA
352 629 1461
www.kipcreative.com
Page 176

Latin Brand
Silvio Giorgi
Juan Gonzalez N35-135 e Ignacio
San Maria, edif. Metropoli, of. 606
Quito
Ecuador
593-2 2461075
www.latin-brand.com
Pages 74–77, 158–159, 177

Lippincott
Connie Birdsall
Brendán Murphy
499 Park Avenue
New York, NY 10022
USA
212 521 0000
www.lippincott.com
Pages 160–161, 176, 177

Mary Hutchison Design LLC
Mary Chin Hutchison
4010 Whitman Ave. N.
Seattle, WA 98103
USA
206 407 3460
www.maryhutchisondesign.com
Page 179

MauriceRedmond.com
Herzogstr 32
80803
Munich
Germany
0049 89 321 68594
www.mauriceredmond.com
Page 178

Sbothra.com
Sanjeev Bothra
C115 Sri Ram Marg, Shyam Nagar,
Jaipur 302019
India
91 141 2292838
www.sbothra.com
Page 183

Sebastiany Branding Design
Renato Akira
Pinheiros, São Paulo SP 05429-030
Brazil
55 11 3926 3937
www.sebastiany.com.br
Page 183

Seltzer Design
Rochelle Seltzer
45 Newbury St., #406
Boston, MA 02116
USA
617 353 0303
www.selterdesign.com
Page 184

Smash Lab
Eric Karjaluoto
403-318 Homer Street
Vancouver, BC V6B 2V2
Canada
604 683 2250
www.smashlab.com
Page 184

Sony Corporation
Tadashi Furuchi
1-7-1 Kounan Minato-ka
Tokyo, 108-0075
Japan
81 3 6748 2111
www.sony.co.jp/design
Pages 144–145, 184

Splash: Design
Phred Martin
106–1441 Ellis St.
Kelowna, BC V1Y 2B3
Canada
250 868 1059
www.splashdesign.biz
Page 184

Spring
Norrie Zaplatynsky
301–1250 Homer Street
Vacouver, BC V6B 1C6
Canada
604 683 0167
www.springadvertising.com
Pages 184, 185

Sterling Brands
Debbie Millman
350 Fifth Avenue, Suite 1714
New York, NY 10118
USA
212 329 4600
www.sterlingbrands.com
Page 185

Studio Blue
Cheryl Towler Weese
800 West Huron
Chicago, IL 60642
USA
312 243 2241
www.studioblue.us
Page 185

Studio International
Boris Ljubicic
Buconjiceva 43 10 000
Zagreb
Croatia
385 1 3760 171
www.studio-international.com
Page 186

Studio Rasic
Marko Rasic
Medulic'eva 1 10000
Zagreb
Croatia
385 1 4847 224
www.studio-rasic.hr
Page 186

Subplot Design Inc.
Roy White
301–318 Homer Street
Vancouver, BC V6B 2V2
Canada
604 685 2990
www.subplot.com
Page 186

Substance 151
Ida Cheinman
2304 E. Baltimore Street
Baltimore, MD 21224
USA
410 732 8379
www.substance151.com
Page 185

Three 76 Design
Bryan McCloskey
612-6400 Coach Hill Rd. SW
Calgary, Alberta T3H 1B8
Canada
403 988 7033
www.three76.com
Page 187

tmarks Design
Terry B. Marks
803 South King Street
Seattle, WA 98104
USA
206 628 6427
www.tmarksdesign.com
Page 186

Turner Duckworth
David Turner
831 Montgomery Street
San Francisco, CA 94133
USA
415 675 7777
www.turnerduckworth.com
Pages 36–41

VSA Partners Inc.
Dana Arnett
Jamie Kovall
1347 South State Street
Chicago, IL 60605
USA
312 895 5054
www.vsapartners.com
Page 187

W Design
Kristy Weyrich
2922 Whidden Street
Boise, ID 83702
USA
208 345 9562
www.wdesignboise.com
Page 187

Weights&Pulleys Ltd.
James Selman
2824 N.W. Thurman Street
Portland, OR 97210
USA
503 546 1520
www.weightsandpulleys.com
Pages 162–165

Wongdoody
Amy Wise
8500 Steller Dr., #5
Culver City, CA 90232
USA
310 280 7918
www.wongdoody.com
Page 187

ABOUT THE AUTHOR

Michael Hodgson (Mick to many) was born and raised in London after World War II. He was lucky to have parents who embraced good design. As part of the postwar generation of newly married couples living in London as it rebuilt itself, there was a positive feeling that welcomed the new and the fresh. His father drove one of the first Mini Minors, after owning several classic Lancia Aurelias.

Michael attended Brighton College of Art where he was influenced by Penny Sparke's inspiring design history classes and introduced to the designers, photographers, and artists featured in books that had been in his parent's flat or outside on the streets of London. Cushions covered in fabrics designed by Robin and Lucienne Day, Reynolds Stone's cover of the Windsor Castle brochure, a coronation mug by Eric Ravilious sat on the living room shelf, and, of course, the work of Eric Gill was everywhere. The book recording the midwife's visits after he was born was set in Gill Sans, and, he later realized, so too were half the signs on any high street.

In his final year at Brighton, he wrote a design thesis entitled "Corporate Madness." The idea grew out of his final year design project, documenting the disappearance of the Southdown Bus Company as it was swallowed by the National Bus Company. After graduating he spent five years at Harpers & Queen, the last two as art director.

In 1979 he moved to Santa Monica, California, to the land of Coca-Cola, baseball, and Steve McQueen—the American icons that had always fascinated him. Since 1998, he has been principal of Santa Monica–based Ph.D, A Design Office, a firm whose design thinking approach is based on the idea of Visual Personalities: capturing the essence and soul of the client, then communicating those qualities throughout all applications from building signage and websites to identities and marketing collateral. When he's not in the office, he can often be found riding his bike in the Santa Monica Mountains. He always, always makes time for tea.

ACKNOWLEDGMENTS

The idea of writing a book must be attractive to a lot of (most) people. It's an ego boost, especially to a designer whose scope of services includes book design. Most are smart enough to stop there and realize that designing is what they do, and that writing books—especially design books—should be left to Steven Heller.

I always counted myself as one of those smart ones, and I had more than one conversation with Rockport's previous editor, Kristin Ellison, in which we both agreed that perhaps writing a book wasn't a good fit for me. Why did I change my mind? A moment of weakness, maybe? Did Emily Potts know me better than her predecessor, or maybe not as well? Whatever happened I said, "Yes" and now I'm thrilled. I am a published author, but not without the help and encouragement of many.

The first being Emily, editor supreme. In my office Alice Joo did all the chasing, emailing, and production and Randy Walker kept everything else going. Matthew Porter learned how to write English and made me look like a great writer. Tony and Rusty, Pam, Susan, Tom, thank you.

Of course, my children Lily, Maudie Rae, and Lucie for their constant inspiration; and Gill for putting up with the long hours and putting up with me!

Thanks to my lovely Mum who continues to inspire us all with her endless youth and energy. The book is dedicated to my Dad.